WHY FIDEL ABANDONED CHE?

ALBERTO MÜLLER

TecnoTur
Publishing
Is there a book inside you?

CONTENTS

Why Fidel abandoned Che?   v

Dedication   ix

Acknowledgments   xi

Prologue by Martín Guevara   1

Introduction   7

1. The Life of Che Guevara (Synthesis)   13
   His encounter with the Cuban revolution

2. First tensions between Fidel and Che   27

3. On the way to the Congo   49
   Conversation with Gamal Abdel Nasser. Fidel makes public his letter of resignation, which upsets Che. Hurried escape from the Congo.

4. Bolivia, a misbegotten objective   80
   The only country in Latin America where peasants were the owners of most of the land. Monje, the Communist that betrayed Che in Bolivia

5. Capture and assassination of Che   104
   Hungry, thirsty, lacking medicines for asthma, and shoeless.

6. The abandonment   130
   Che cast a very large shadow over Fidel. Reasons for the abandonment. Poem to Jesus Christ

Documents and Notes   155

Bibliography   201

About the Author   211

WHY FIDEL ABANDONED CHE?

AN ESSAY BY ALBERTO MÜLLER,
CUBAN WRITER

«Never did I see myself so alone again in all my journey.»

Che Guevara (*Congo Diary*)

Why Fidel abandoned Che

by Alberto Müller

First edition published in English.

English translation: Frank Rodríguez

Published by: TecnoTur Publishing

Editing and internal layout: Allan Tépper

Cover design: Karla Herrera

ISBN of the paperback:

979-8-9925106-2-1

ISBN of the electronic version (ebook):

979-8-9925106-3-8

ISBN of the audiobook:

979-8-9925106-4-5

To my inseparable wife Tensy, who has, for more than five years, put up with patience my almost schizoid journalistic investigative obsession surrounding the death of Che Guevara in Bolivia.

To my close friend Octavio de la Concepción de la Pedraja, alias, Tavito, Moro, Morogoro, El Médico and Muganga, who died along Che Guevara in the mountains of Bolivia and who accompanied him as well in the guerrilla campaign in the Congo.

Tavito, as we called him at the University of Havana and in the halls of the Catholic University Organization, was always a loyal friend, an exemplary Christian, and a tireless fighter against the dictatorship of Fulgencio Batista in Cuba. His death along with Che, abandoned in the Bolivian mountains, doesn't remove the mystery or my pain at his distant death within the ranks of the Communist process that has distanced Cuba from freedom.

To all my Cuban compatriots, men and women, who have fought to make Cuba a more just and free country.

Alberto Müller

ACKNOWLEDGMENTS

I must especially thank Juan Manuel Salvat for his suggestions, comments and permanent encouragement; to Adrianne Miller, the Cuban US-American writer who inspired me to have this book published in English; to my friend Martín Guevara (nephew of Che Guevara) who wrote the prologue of this essay and finally to my editor Felipe Lázaro and his publishing house Betania in Spain for co-editing the second edition in the original language.

My permanent gratitude to them for making it possible for this essay *Why Fidel abandoned Che*.

PROLOGUE BY MARTÍN GUEVARA

T he officer in charge of operations once again came into the room, which had only one air vent, where a lifeless body lay next to a wounded man who was at the limit of human or animal endurance, although still conscious, sitting, and with a tired, though firm look in his eyes. The officer and the prisoner heard once again a burst of shots in the room next door; the next-to-last man had just been executed. The officer, who had held long conversations with the prisoner as a means of interrogating him, had tried to fulfill the wishes of his superiors to have the prisoner transferred to Panamá alive, however, this time he came into that somber death room to inform him of the decision reached regarding his disposition:

-«*Commander, in a few moments a soldier will come in and he will proceed to shoot you.*»

They looked at each other standing, then, the guerrilla chief gave him the last belongings he still had, and they gave each other a military salute, and then the prisoner told him:

--«*Perhaps it's for the best.*»

The officer left, the soldier came in, and began to speak incoherently while the guerrilla chief, wearing rags and with skin hanging from his ribs, just about to leave behind his asthma for good, told him:

--«*Go on, I know what you are here to do.*»

Then the soldier let out several deadly shots, including one that cut across his forearm. Expecting never to see this body again, and in order to remember it for a long time, the high-ranking officer cleaned up its face with a wet handkerchief, trying to close its eyes, but they remained stubbornly open.

Ernesto Guevara de La Serna died at La Higuera in such conditions of squalor and defeat that it symbolized an ode to desolation.

To everyone, the man who was dying, consistent with his ideas, and who, depending on one's point of view --his enemies thinking he had paid for his crimes of violence, his friends and sympathizers that he had been raised to the mythical level of a superior being, while impartial historians could see the extreme of exhaustion, of loyalty to his ideas, of obstinacy, and the high price of errors-- all of them, in one way or another, if observing events from a realistic point of view, will not be able to avoid being accosted by an overwhelming amount of signs, which, when taken together, point to more than a suspicion but rather to the almost naked truth of a surreptitious story of consummate treason. A victory of pragmatism over Utopia.

The rest is part of History, of mythology, of one of the legends of the 20st century that each interprets from the place where life has placed each, from the ideological sensibility that reached the hypothalamus of almost the totality of the active population of those years, on one side of the issue or the other.

With great objectivity and in a deep work of research, this work by Alberto Müller offers us a point of view, removed of all prejudice, of all ideological veneer, from which not only light can be shed upon this historic episode, but also upon the generalized abandonment he was object of by the supposed comrades-in-arms of one of the most committed men of the Cuban revolution, and paradoxically of international Communism, which deserted him.

The richness of this work in associating ideas, in its perception of the points where truth and truthfulness meet, where fraud and intentionality join up, the seriousness of the bibliography, the nobleness of its goal, make this book a key source to delve deeper into clarification, into the search for answers in one of the most fundamental episodes in the History of the 20th century.

I met its author, Alberto Müller, through our common friend Adrianne Miller, and ever since we exchanged our first words, I realized that I was in front of a person of integrity, somebody that not only doesn't fear truth but who seeks it, someone of deep democratic values. And even more, a man of Christian values, that an atheist as I can recognize a mile away, regardless of where they may be.

We talked some years back about the perceptions each of us have of the Cuban revolution, his personal story, mine, the work that I was then doing about my life in the midst of that whirlwind, in that sampler of the most diverse machinations, mechanical and political, if that is a name that can be given to that ensemble of technicisms and presdigitation to sustain a group in power for the maximum amount of time possible, without any other substrata, sustenance, or common denominator except one, their permanence in power.

We talked of years of prison, about the noble sentiments that move him today towards Cuba and towards the common people, who are in the end the ones that suffer the whims of bus drivers on the bus of History, when these, by grabbing the steering wheel, turn the wheel towards a dead end, jumping over a whole group of codes and rules on the way.

We also talked about me, and, of course, about my uncle, Che Guevara. Of the impact and weight he had in my life, of the things I admire about him, and those I reject, about what they tried to sell us as a model.

What I was able to offer to our conversation were points of view, certainties born of a sixth sense, in the indefinite dimension called a hunch or a suspicion, but that at times has more weight than many testimonials.

When I was born, my uncle had already left Argentina for the last time, and he had already met Raúl and Fidel Castro, and Fidel had already converted several times to various convictions, confessions, different doctrines, he had already been a Jesuit, Orthodox, Authentic, democrat, revolutionary, then Communist, and then I was born, and then later he had time to convert to many other things, and now he is even walking in the path of defender of the Chinese Revolution in exchange for valued sustenance; and although I had not had the opportunity to spend time with my uncle, at least not in the commonly accepted chronological way, in fact I did with the energy that his specter left on the family's cosmogony, in addition to his official omnipresence, or rather the use of him, his life, and especially his death, exploited by Fidel once he was not a problem any longer.

I was surprised by the generosity of the author of this book to place himself above pettiness, having put skin in the game and having suffered not a few hardships in the hands of little-tolerant post-revolutionary enthusiasm, while still being able to see things from the impartial angle of someone writing History, even as one filled with the noblest feeling, when he could easily feel the most ardent hatred. This really caught my attention.

He seemed to me so authentic, so courageous, so objective, leading me to consider it an honor to have the possibility to be counted among his friends.

But not even so, could I surmise the surprise that overtook

me when mixing enjoyment with responsibility when I read this book.

The association of ideas, the reconstruction of links to glance at the direction of the moorage in which these events took place, the offering of names of revolutionary militants who more than surprised were sold out by the sudden turn that their common project took, the struggle against the Batista dictatorship, all constitute valuable aspects of this book.

In my way of thinking, the goal of a work is what provides it the highest level. The honor and the achievement of this book lies in its search for the truth of a time period very much in the present, although it appears to be chronologically in the past, yet based on the principles of truth, justice and humanism.

I must also say that these same principles are what make me feel proud to have been selected to write the prologue of this valuable book, as the whole world needs to delve deeper into coexistence, tolerance, and the construction of peace, and so any opportunity to add a grain of sand to that cause, is for me the greatest of honors.

May this book contribute to achieve the amity that will be needed in large measure in a Cuba wounded by division and the erosion of fundamental values, which will only be achieved with the participation of all parties, and with truth in a protagonistic role.

Martín Guevara

(Nephew of Che Guevara)

INTRODUCTION

Any facet of the life of Ernesto Guevara, due to the historical dimension of this figure, is never an easy task for any researcher.

It's important to emphasize that we were not seeking to write a biography, but rather that we were focusing on something that seemed revealing and fascinating to a journalist and writer scrutinizing reality with the eye of a researcher.

Che Guevara's time in Bolivia turned out to be a long succession of mishaps, indiscipline, betrayals and abandonments, which, without devaluing the commitment and zeal of the protagonists to reach a particular political objective in Latin America, lead inevitably to the failure of the guerilla project and to the death of most of its participants, including Che.

Those that ordered the death or execution of Ernesto Guevara at La Higuera, without prejudice, violated all the existing codes of war and military ethics, not realizing that with this criminal act they were turning the Argentine-Cuban guerrilla into a long-lasting myth.

When these same Bolivian military men, additionally ordered his hands cut off in an unusual act of physical mutilation, they gave wings for this new revolutionary myth to ascend into unheard of heights, and for youthful popular imagination to accept it with veneration, as a new never-before-seen icon of recent history. And so it has been, although for some it may not be fair or justified.

Academics of Cuban history will need to decipher with great critical rigor the reasons why the General Intelligence Directorate (DGI) of the Cuban revolutionary government authorized, or gave its approval, for the Congo and Bolivia to be the places or countries for Che Guevara to develop his revolutionary projects by continuing with one of the most widely known master ideas of Leon Trotsky, «the permanent revolution» in favor of the proletariat and of the exploited, when none of the two geographical theaters, in distant continents, presented the minimal security conditions required for the successful development of these guerrilla projects.

If the experience of sending a group of Cuban revolutionaries to the Congo «is the story of a failure» according to the words of Che Guevara in the first phrase of his book Congo Diary, it would be interesting to know how Che would represent his own death in Bolivia.

Che was to die, to his personal bitterness and suffering, abandoned, hungry, without asthma medicines, wearing rags tied to his feet, as he had lost his boots, and according to the testimony of most of his biographers, with hardly the wish to continue fighting the enemy.

At the time of his death, paradoxically, the two great intelligence agencies in the world —the CIA in the U.S. and the KGB in the Soviet Union, who had been involved in a struggle of confrontation, infiltrations and double agents everywhere— were in agreement about the need to physically eliminate or neutralize the activities of Ernesto «Che» Guevara.

And that is another of the questions that this journalistic narrative tries to bring to mind for all interested in this piece of contemporary history.

It will also stimulate the study of these events, which tie into the interest of the CIA and the KGB to take out Che from the political revolutionary scene of the time.

This real historical framework could reveal that on the day after the confirmation of the death of Che at La Higuera, Bolivia, both agencies would feel satisfied and relieved. We don't know if they shook hands or if they exchanged congratulatory messages.

Up to now, the most important fact known about this sacrificial event is that the Central Intelligence Agency (CIA) did all that was humanly possible with the Bolivian government to avoid Guevara's death.

This book is also strictly animated by two timely events: one is the Diary of Che in Bolivia, whose reading uncovers without compunctions the state of abandonment that occasioned Che's capture and his death at La Higuera.

The comment, so often and insistently repeated in Che's Bolivian Diary (Diario del Che) during the last six months of his life, «We have lost contact with Manila,» or «We continue to be unable to reestablish contact with Manila,» or «Morale is very low because we have no contact with Manila,» is akin to a melancholy and accusatory refrain that should strike the conscience of any human anywhere in the world, and above all when we realize that Manila stands for the Cuban revolutionary government, or more precisely, Fidel Castro.

The other stimulus that led me to write this book is a personal one, and it has to do with the loyalty the author holds from his youthful days at the Havana University for his friend Octavio de la Concepción de la Pedraja, alias Tavito, El Moro, Morogoro, Muganga or El Médico who was a member of Che's guerrilla.

In one of his last conversations with the author, Tavito told the author that the Cuban revolution would not be Communist but rather nationalist, and as Cuban as are royal palms, asking from him trust, time and understanding. To which the author reassured his friend that if in fact the Cuban revolution turned out not to take the Communist route, then both of them would once again find each other in the same stage of the Cuban Revolution.

Later on history marched in another direction and Morogoro or Tavito died along with Che in the mountains of Bolivia, the Cuban revolution declared itself Communist, and lined up under the political handling of the Soviets, and so the two friends never physically met again.

This essay tries to carefully link the chain of events that struck down Che Guevara and his group of Cuban guerrillas in Bolivia.

In this manner, we will better understand this dramatic piece of Latin American history, that some have tried to alter or hide, which demonstrates, without compunctions, how Che Guevara and his Cuban guerrillas died in the Bolivian mountains, abandoned, hungry, thirsty, and in the case of Che, in rags and without his own boots or asthma medicine.

The book is nonetheless bold and ambitious at the same time, because it follows the steps in the Congo, Egypt, China, Moscow, Prague and finally Bolivia, among other corners of lesser importance, of a man of extensive historical dimensions, as was Ernesto (Che) Guevara.

Alberto Müller

1

THE LIFE OF CHE GUEVARA
(SYNTHESIS)
HIS ENCOUNTER WITH
THE CUBAN REVOLUTION

Che was proud of his family. He had acute asthma
since childhood. Identified with the poor and
lepers. Visits Argentina and Latin America.

«Today begins a new stage.»
(Diary of Che, November 1966)

Cuban, Antonio «Ñico» López, who had been a
member of the assault team against the Moncada
Barracks in Santiago de Cuba along with Fidel
Castro and the other revolutionaries of the July 26th Movement in 1953, was the one to give Ernesto Guevara de la Serna
the nickname of «Che» when both met during the revolt in
Guatemala in 1954, when the Cuban thought it funny that

Guevara would use that «che» expression with great frequency in his speech.

Ernesto Guevara was born on June 14, 1928 in the city of Rosario, Argentina, and all his family members would affectionately identify him with the moniker of «Teté». Family testimonies express —with a certain amount of certainty— that his actual birth occurred a year before, but that the parents didn't want to register him in the city or municipal records as at the time of the child's conception, they were not legally married, and that is why both left the city for a while.

His mother Celia de la Serna, came from a family of lineage and aristocratic aspirations, educated in a Catholic school for high society girls –The Sacred Heart– which made her consider —during her teenage years— about the possibility of a religious or convent life. With the passage of time, Celia would abandon her religious beliefs to turn into an activist revolutionary committed to the defense of her son Ernesto, whom she adored with maternal passion. The father of the child, Ernesto Guevara Lynch, was an extroverted and likeable businessman who would chase skirts left and right. This behavior caused frequent issues in his marriage with his wife. It is known, through the testimony of family members, that Celia de la Serna's family had opposed her marriage to Ernesto Guevara Lynch, considering him emotionally unstable and irresponsible from the financial point of view.

From a very early age, the child suffered strong asthma attacks, product of an acute bronchial pneumonia, for which his father Ernesto blamed Celia, the mother of the child, for having brought on the asthma by bathing the child when he was very little in the cold waters of a river. [1]

The persistent asthma ailment explains the personality of the child, who from a very early age had a tendency to escape the family environment, hiding from his parents, and being surly with his friends, although on the other hand, he liked to play chess at times with his father during leisure moments also showing traits of respect and deep love for his mother Celia.

At school, the child applied himself reading adventure and travel books, studying the works of Horacio Quiroga, Charles Baudelaire and Sigmund Freud and enjoyed reciting and memorizing by heart the verses by Pablo Neruda. Poetry, both reading and writing it, was becoming his preferred literary genre.

During his adolescence, he delved deeper into studying the life of Leon Trotsky and other personalities of the 20th century Russian revolution. This trend explains how Ernesto, already a teenager in his new social environment –once the family had moved to the city of Alta Gracia-- enrolled in the Committee to Aid the Spanish Republic. In his youthful years, Guevara continued to suffer from asthma and began to develop a mindset of commiseration for the poor, the ill, the most needy and lepers. In records of the Argentine Army, it is noted that Ernesto Guevara de la Serna was «diminished in

---

1.   *Constenla*, Julia. Celia, la Madre del Che, Editorial Debolsillo, 2008 / p. 27.

physical capabilities», a reason that led to his discharge from mandatory military service. [2]

FIRST TRIP THROUGH SOUTH AMERICA

In the middle of this emotional crossroads, he made his first motorcycle trip through Latin America with his close friend, Alberto Granado, in an adventurous attempt to tour and to get to know different regions and cities in the Americas, including the possibility of reaching countries such as Venezuela and the United States. The two left Córdoba on December 29, 1951 on a motorcycle they called *La Poderosa II* (*The Powerful II*). The trip by the two friends began with a frustrating emotional experience for Guevara when they made a stop in Miramar Beach where his girlfriend Chinchina Ferreira was spending her vacation with an aunt.

Guevara wanted to extract a commitment of loyalty from Ferreira, but he was unsuccessful, as she ended up rejecting him without the possibility of reconsidering her decision, although friends of both state that they felt true emotional attraction and mutual love.

The young Chinchina told her friend Miriam Urrutia about this incident:

«He saw me as an impediment to the life of the adventurer he wanted to be. He felt trapped and he wanted to free himself, and I must have been an obstacle to this. I don't know where he wanted to go; he wanted to leave and travel the world.»

---

2.   Ortega, Luis. *Yo soy el Che*, Ediciones Espuela de Plata, 2009 / p. 29

In addition, the young Ernesto Guevara demanded of Chinchina another proof of love, asking the girl for her bracelet to take as a souvenir of the beloved object of his love on his Latin American trip, but she refused to hand it over without any hesitation.

From the Argentine beach of Miramar, the two friends went on with their trip and a few days later they entered Chile, where they had an intense social experience with lepers in Valparaíso.

Then they reached Valdivia, and as they were leaving this city on their Poderosa II, the engine of the vehicle gave out and the travelers found themselves without their precious transportation for the long journey they had planned throughout the continent.

From Valdivia, they used different means to reach the copper mine of Chuquicamata in Tacna, the largest open-sky mine in the world, run by a US-American company.

According to most of Guevara biographers, a pair of Communist miners in the Chuquicamata mine in Chile would leave permanent imprints on the political education of the young Guevara by emotionally bringing him closer to the Marxist revolutionary model.[3]

These Communist friends seem to have fed and encouraged in Guevara first a hatred for the United States and later his

---

3.   Castañeda, Jorge G. *La vida en rojo*, Alfaguara, 1997 / pp. 74 – 76

revolutionary radicalism, which he is to later state in his diary of notes:

«The stiff couple in the desert night, hugging, was the very representation of the proletariat in any part of the world. They didn't even have a blanket to cover up, and so we gave them a sample of human solidarity, while Alberto and I covered up with the other one.»

During the month of April, they visited Cuzco, capital of the Inca Empire, and the imperial city of Machu Picchu. Then they departed for the city of Abancay, where they visited the leprosarium in Huambo.

From here the two friends, by now May 1952, arrived in Lima, Perú, where they met Dr. Hugo Pesce, who would exert a significant influence on the lives of both, and to whom Guevara later on would dedicate his book *Guerrilla Warfare*. The dedication of the book goes as follows:

«To Dr. Hugo Pesce, who, perhaps unknowingly, provoked a great change in my attitude towards life and society, with the same adventurous spirit of always, but channeled towards objectives more harmonious to the needs of the Americas.» [4]

In Lima, once one of his worst asthmatic crises in the whole trip is overcome, Che and Granado visited a leprosarium on the outskirts of the capital where their friend Pesce worked.

From here they embarked for Iquitos visiting the

---

4. O'Donell, Pacho: *La vida por un mundo mejor CHE*, Editorial Debolsillo, 2005. / p.75

leprosarium of San Pablo, on the banks of the Amazon River, where the doctors there provided them with a raft to continue on their journey.

A distinctive trait of the two travelers was therefore their affection for lepers, brought about by the professional experience and sentiments of Alberto Granado, who for many years of his work life had tended to these types of illnesses.

Everything seems to indicate that in this first phase of his journey, Guevara was more interested in visiting leprosaria that in researching archeological formations or about politics, by virtue of the humanitarian influence that his friend had exerted on him, although he would still assimilate social and humanitarian experiences during certain moments of the trip, such as was the case with the miners at the Chuquicamata mine.

In addition to Perú, they visited Bolivia, Colombia and Venezuela, by now aboard trucks and odd means of transportation, after their bike had gone to motorcycle heaven. While at the Andes Range, they went through their worst mishap of all the trajectory and Guevara's asthma became aggravated due to the climate.

There are even many credible references from before 1950 regarding a trip that Ernesto Guevara took on a motorbike throughout Argentina, where he visited the leprosarium in the north of Córdoba, where his friend Alberto Granado worked.

Some of his biographers affirm that asthma was the main impediment to the development of an emotionally balanced personality in Ernesto Guevara. Asthma was the reason for his rejection from obligatory army service in his country. In the end, it will be his commitment to fight against social injustices and against the policy of the United States that would move him towards revolutionary extremism, despite his physical limitations.

Guevara showed in his early years —after leaving behind his adolescence— that he needed to find other roads in the world, far from Argentina, far from his family and far from his teenage classmates.

Some observers and academics of psychology, such as author Adrianne Miller, attach this tendency to travel and to disappear to the periphery, away from his family, to be the real leitmotif or driving force in the life of Ernesto Guevara.[5]

This road finally seems to find him with the Cuban revolution, in guerrilla fronts and in violence as a model for action.

Guevara proceeded in his journey through South America reaching Colombia, but due to the dictatorship of Laureano Gómez, his friends advised him to go on his way, and so he reached Venezuela in 1952.

During his stay in Caracas, his friend Alberto Granado got a job in a leprosarium due to his friendship with Dr. Hugo Pesce.

---

5. Interview with Adrianne Miller, writer and psychologist.

At this time, Guevara decided to return to Argentina to finish up his medical studies, which some say ended in April 1953. By the same token, other sources close to his family state with certainty that he was never able to get a medical diploma. By now, the asthma that he had suffered as a child had become Guevara's inseparable sidekick, a man who in this first stage carried his revolutionary sensibility on his back, but his thirst for adventure and his wish to be a poet and to serve lepers was even stronger within him. The impetus of a new trip throughout the American continent shows Guevara's evolution with a marked political awareness, though not abandoning his preferences for archeology, with asthma always lurking about.

SECOND TRIP THROUGH THE AMERICAS

Guevara began this second trip in July 1953, accompanied by his childhood friend Carlos Ferrer. The goal of the trip was to reach Caracas to join up with his other friend Alberto Granado.

The first stop on the train ride was in La Paz, Bolivia, where they remained for several weeks. In this city, Guevara became favorably impressed with the Agrarian Reform of the Revolutionary Nationalist Movement, designed by the President of the Republic, Víctor Paz Estensoro, who had distributed lands among the peasants, setting a precedent for social justice in Latin America, trying to close the path of local oligarchs and Communists, who were more interested in political power and in nationalizing the means of production than in granting land to indigenous farmers and peasants.

Guevara then describes in his daily notes in Bolivia as the «Shanghai of the Americas» due to the rainbow of business-people and travelers from different origins and countries that were coming to that country in search of fortune.

Knowing about this social land distribution in Bolivia, some analysts may be asking, how is it that Ernesto Guevara accepts years later to open up a guerrilla front in that Latin American country, once the disaster that he starred in the Congo, Africa had ended, knowing that the peasants – mostlty landowners now– were not a marginalized or exploited class in Bolivia?

Next, the two friends travelled to Perú, visiting the cities of Puno, Cuzco and Machu Picchu, to finally make a stop in Lima, where they met once again with Dr. Hugo Pesce.

From Perú they travelled to Ecuador, where they met up with their leftist friend Ricardo Rojo. Later they travelled to Panamá and Costa Rica, where they met the leftist political leader Juan Bosch and Manuel Mora Valverde, a Communist Costa Rican.

They planned to visit Honduras with the goal of seeing the ruins of the Chortís in Copán, but since they were unable to get a visa, they travelled to Guatemala to visit the Mayan ruins of Quiriguá.

By this time, Guevara's adventurism began to transform gradually into a revolutionary scheme in search of new horizons of struggle.

On December 24, 1953 Ernesto Guevara reached Guatemala and met Hilda Gadea, who would become his first wife, his economic protector, and the one to drive him ideologically to bury his spontaneous interest in archeology and poetry. Guevara then began to consolidate in his mind the way of Marxist revolutionary struggle.

His friendship with a group of Cuban exiles in Guatemala at the time gave him the definitive orientation that he needed, so that for the first time he paused to think about the armed path as an instrument in revolutionary struggle.

The violent overthrow of Jacobo Arbenz in the convulsive Guatemala of 1954 by the country's political right with the support of the U.S. Central Intelligence Agency (CIA), not only caused Guevara to see the nature of political violence but also drove him to prioritize the importance of revolutionary violence throughout his life, now for the sake of Marxist ideals.

On September 18th of that year, he decided to leave Guatemala, crossing the border and arriving in México a few days later. Hilda Gadea would be momentarily left behind in his life, as Guevara had the undisclosed intention of never being with her again, since he really didn't have any feelings of love for her.

In México City, Guevara again met his friend Ñico López

who encouraged him to join the plans to organize an armed movement in Cuba.

In June 1955, he met Raúl Castro, when the latter arrived in México, and a few days later he met Fidel Castro in this same place. His commitment to the Cuban revolutionary cause was sealed by the feeling of trust that the Cuban leader engendered in the psyche of the adventurer and revolutionary Ernesto Guevara.

Once his political relationship and friendship with Fidel Castro was consolidated, the young Ernesto Guevara was ready to begin his lifelong revolutionary journey, with the new identification as Che.

During the time he was connected with the Cuban revolution, he participated in a series of events impregnated with violent revolutionary acts, radicalizations and travels to distant international meetings representing the revolutionary Cuba of 1959. His earlier nickname of «Teté» is now reserved only for his mother and close relatives.

His life as a high-ranking leader of the Cuban revolution, as minister of various dependencies and as President of the National Bank were really short-lived, because by 1964 he had resigned his naturalized Cuban citizenship when he became aware of his irreconcilable differences with the Soviet Union, which inexorably separated him from Fidel Castro and his revolutionary government.

In these first years of the Cuban revolution, while Che Guevara was the military chief of La Cabaña Fortress in

Havana, the death by firing squad of military members of the Fulgencio Batista dictatorship there becomes for many analysts of his revolutionary wanderings the darkest and most bloody event of his life.

It is curious that despite Guevara's habit of jotting down all the events of his life, the scenes of repeated firing squads at Havana's La Cabaña Fortress go unreported in his notes and diaries.

Four years later, Che Guevara decided to leave Cuba permanently, once he had broken ties with the Soviet Union, comparing the USSR with the aggressiveness and contempt that U.S. imperialism held for the underdeveloped nations of the world, according to his speech in Algiers in April, 1964.

The General Intelligence Directorate (DGI) of the Cuban revolutionary government then organized a guerrilla front in the Congo, which according to Che Guevara's notes and commentary had the objective of supporting the nationalist and revolutionary ideas of murdered Congolese leader Patrice Lumumba. The resounding failure of this guerrilla operation conducted by Che leads to his clandestine exile in Prague.

Later he is to return to Cuba to silently begin preparations and training for the group of Cuban guerrillas that would join him in his last war mission in Bolivian territory. At this time, he would experience a fatal disagreement, namely treason by Mario Monje and the Bolivian Communist Party of his guerrilla project in the mountains of Bolivia, concluding with his death at La Higuera, Bolivia on October 8, 1967.[6]

The most obvious pathology in Ernesto Guevara de la Serna, in this casual summary we have made about his life, is, without a doubt, the acute asthma that followed him almost implacably since childhood, not discounting the importance of his radical vocation as a revolutionary that began with his visit to the Chuquicamata mine.

Che demonstrated throughout the actions of his revolutionary life that he preferred to be compared to Leon Trostky than to Joseph Stalin. And having this existential obsession with permanent revolution he found his death at La Higuera, Bolivia.

---

6. Lee Anderson, John. *Che Guevara*, Grove Press, New York, 1997 / pp. 641 – 643

2

FIRST TENSIONS
BETWEEN FIDEL AND CHE

The Algiers Speech: Che criticizes the Soviets.

Moral incentives. Psychopathologies about the center and the periphery.

«Socialist countries have the moral duty of liquidating their tacit complicity with the exploiting countries of the West.»

(Quote from the speech by Che Guevara in Algiers, 1964)

Che Guevara, like Fidel Castro, set forth the creation of revolutionary focal points at the beginning of the Cuban revolution from the eastern mountain range of Sierra Maestra, with the goal of extending the guerrilla movement to the Sierra Cristal range in the north of Oriente Province, and later on to the mountains of the Escambray Range, in the central part of Cuba, and on to Pinar del Río in the west.

However, paradoxically, the next steps to create revolutionary focal points in the Congo, Africa, and in Ñancahuazú, Bolivia, as the main goal of extending the revolution to other regions of the world became a resounding failure for Che Guevara and for those that were proposing international guerrilla movements in other regions of the planet.

The guerrilla tactics set forth by Che Guevara in his book *Guerrilla Warfare* imply enforcing revolutionary command with an iron hand in the mountains on a small nucleus of guerrillas, who would slowly begin to gain recognition — militarily and politically— within the peasant population, this thus becoming a stimulus or alternative for the development of a mass movement to produce the overthrow of the regime being fought.

In order for this to develop, the author of the book presented several basic conditions: «First of all, one needs to establish who are the fighters in a guerrilla war: on one hand we have the nucleus of oppressors and its agent, the professional army, well-armed and disciplined, which, in many cases, may count on foreign support as well as from a small bureaucratic nucleus, all under the umbrella of the oppressive nucleus.

On the other hand is the population of the nation or region where the guerrilla nucleus is developed. It is important to highlight that the guerrilla struggle, according to Guevara's ideas, is a mass struggle, it is a fight by the people: the guerrilla, as an armed nucleus, is the combative vanguard of the people, and its strength comes from the mass of the population.» That was Guevara's thesis.[1]

This theoretical conception of the «theory of focal points» called *foquismo* in Castilian (aka «Spanish»), set forth by Che, became entrenched in the Congo as in Bolivia, with the variant that in none of these two distant regions did the population enthusiastically join the original imported guerrilla nucleus.

The same thing happened in Salta, Argentina, in a project tied to Che Guevara, which ended up in another failure due to lack of support from the population.

It may be worthwhile to add, as we shall see later in the development of this research work, that in these three cases, in the populations of Salta (1963), Congo (1964) and Bolivia (1966), not only the peasants and natives of the area not join the guerrillas but also ended up rejecting the actors and the essence itself of the project. And this rejection opens up a disturbing question about the theory of guerrilla warfare focal points.

In the Cuban case (1956-1958), once a guerrilla group had become established and developed in the Sierra Maestra Mountains, under the leadership of Fidel Castro, it became critical for the development of that guerrilla front to gain the support of the peasants in this mountainous region as well as to count on the revolutionary activism of the 26th of July

---

1. Guevara, Ernesto. *Guerrilla Warfare*, Nebraska Press, 1998 / pp. 7-14

Movement in the cities, led by Frank País, as well as the rejection of the Cuban dictatorship installed on March 10, 1952.

This activism in the cities developed a civic resistance movement that became organized in all regions and towns in the Island, turning into the main driving force of the revolutionary fronts in reaching their triumph on January 1, 1959.

It is significant that the success obtained in Cuba with the overthrow of the dictatorship of Fulgencio Batista, on account of the joining of civic resistance and the development of guerrilla fronts in the Sierra Maestra (1956-1959), led by Fidel Castro, was never repeated in the later experiences of Che Guevara, which we have just recounted.

In the case of the Cuban experience, we need to take into account the existence of two sectors within the July 26th Movement, called «the plains and the mountains» or «*el llano y la sierra*» which together triggered the decisive push that neutralized and weakened the survival possibilities of the 1952 dictatorship ending with its overthrow on December 31, 1958. Although during the development of the Cuban revolution against the government of Batista, a few political tensions emerged between both groups –the hills and the plains- having its worse moment or climax of greatest tension when some cadres close to Frank País, including his brother Agustín País, accused Vilma Espín (Raúl Castro's future wife) of being the informer that led to Frank's assassination, who was the number one leader of the movement in Santiago de Cuba, on July 30, 1957.

But despite this controversial question, left for future historians to decipher, which is not the subject of this present work, there is no doubt that the combined effort of both factors, together with the arms embargo established by the U.S. Government against the Government of Fulgencio Batista in 1958, created the conditions for the revolutionary triumph on January 1, 1959.

It is necessary to state that the method of the revolutionary «focal point» was successful within the framework of the Cuban revolution, because it had the solidarity of wide sectors of the Cuban middle class, the students, the workers and the peasants, circumstances we shall develop in this chapter.

It's worthwhile to highlight that the guerrilla groups in the Sierra Maestra Range, the Sierra de Cristal Range, the Escambray Range, and the Sierra de los Órganos Range during all the process of the Cuban revolution, led by Fidel, his brother Raúl, Che Guevara, Ramiro Valdés, Juan Almeida, Húber Matos, Camilo Cienfuegos, Eloy Gutiérrez Menoyo and Rolando Cubelas, to name just the most renowned rebel commanders, counted on the scant wish to fight of Batista's own army, lacking the morale to fight due to the government corruption prevalent in official spheres.

Among the most important leaders that acted in the plains, associated with the 26th of July Movement were Frank País, Vilma Espín, Faustino Pérez, Carlos Franqui, Haydée Santamaría Cuadrado, Armando Hart, René Ramos Latour (Daniel), Manolo Ray, David Salvador and Felipe Pazos, among others, most of Social Democrat or Christian Socialist revolutionary tendencies, with a more open vision of society than the one being bandied about by the Sierra Maestra guerrillas, with the exception of Húber Matos, who never held central statist or authoritarian notions as were being proclaimed by the more radical or extremists elements in the Sierra, some already with Marxist training, as was the case of Ernesto Guevara and Raúl Castro.[2]

To this dichotomy of the plains and the mountains in the struggle of the Cuban revolution against the dictatorship of Fulgencio Batista, one needs to add the presence of the March 13 Directorate (Directorio 13 de Marzo), a movement born on the campus of the University of Havana under the leadership of José Antonio Echeverría, President of the FEU, the Federation of College Students, a Catholic activist who died in action on March 13, 1957 trying to execute dictator Fulgencio Batista.

It is also important to highlight in this piece of Cuban history that we are trying to understand the trip to México by José Antonio Echeverría in the month of August 1956 together with fellow students Fructuoso Rodríguez and Faure Chomón, to coordinate unity plans with Fidel Castro and the July 26th Movement, with the goal of establishing the guerrilla war and support for the landing of the yacht Granma about to launch from a Mexican port.

There are reports of a negative reaction on the part of Echev-

_____

2. Franqui, Carlos. *Retrato de familia con Fidel*, Editorial Seix Barral, 1981 / pp. 40-42

and his colleagues when they realize, to their surprise, that Fidel Castro had an egocentric and ambitious personality.[3]

This negative perception regarding Fidel Castro, shared widely by his classmates in the university revolutionary movement, including Frank País, who was also present at the meeting in México, is decisive in trying to understand some later events in the development of the Cuban revolution.

Echeverría would return to Havana disheartened regarding the personality and authoritarian character of Fidel Castro, which makes some believe that this is where the idea to organize an attack against the Presidential Palace to liquidate dictator Fulgencio Batista. in collaboration with revolutionary groups belonging to the Partido Auténtico, led by its leader Menelao Mora, had its genesis.

To the existing differences between cadres in the plains and in the hills within the 26th of July Movement, now is added the differences between the leaders of the Sierra Maestra and those of the University Directorate.

When Echeverría, Mora and other revolutionaries died in an attempt to shoot dictator Fulgencio Batista in the attack on the Presidential Palace on March 13, 1957, from the Sierra Maestra, Fidel Castro directly assumed a critical position defining publicly the heroic action by the University Directorate «as a putsch against the Cuban revolution of the Sierra Maestra.»

---

3. Fernández León, Julio. *José A. Echeverría*, Ediciones Universal, 2007 / pp. 385-393

This opinion, issued from the Sierra Maestra less than a month after the revolutionary event that tried to execute dictator Batista inside his government house, shows the harshness with which Fidel Castro was able to treat any strategy that was independent of the revolutionary front strategy that he espoused.

These differences will become essential later in order to understand the early opposition of revolutionary elements against the centralized and authoritarian tendencies of Fidel Castro in the first few years after the triumph of the revolution (1959 - 1961).

After the triumph of January 1, 1959 over the dictatorship of Batista (1952-1958), with the dictator's precipitous flight, Che Guevara kept up his loyalty to Mao's revolutionary focal point theory, and to Trotsky's permanent state of revolution, while Fidel Castro began to make friendly moves with a certain amount of urgency towards the Soviet Union in search of concessions, economic subsidies and arms, something he is to achieve in short order.[4]

The insertion of Cuba into the scenario of the Cold War begins then, under the protective umbrella of the Soviet Union, an incipient process at the time, which ends up separating Che Guevara from the Communist Cuba of Fidel Castro, as we will analyze in the rest of this book.

At this juncture in 1959, a situation developed in Cuba which

---

4. Blasier, Cole. *The Hovering Giant*, University of Pittsburgh, 1985 / pp. 195-200

was similar to the one that took place during the Bolshevik revolution of 1922, when Joseph Stalin gained power and Trotsky accused him of being the «undertaker of the revolution» and when Vladimir Lenin himself alerted of the great dangers to the Russian revolution of electing Stalin to the number one spot in the party.

Stalin, without much hesitation began the obscure process of quenching with blood the internal democracy in the Bolshevik Party and in this fashion, became a great dictator. In that process, revolutionary leaders of the stature of Trotsky, Kamenev and Bugarin, just to mention some of the most visible heads, gradually disappeared from the scene.[5]

In a singular parallelism and with his own style, Fidel Castro crushed the democracy promised by the revolution, costing the lives or political prison –in those early years– of the main non-Communist leaders of the Cuban revolution, such as Humberto Sorí Marín, Huber Matos and Porfirio Ramírez, all commanders of the Rebel Army.

Initially, in economic matters, both Fidel Castro and his brother Raúl and Che Guevara championed in Cuba what academic and economist Carmelo Mesa Lago calls the first idealist cycle of the economy (1959-1966) in the Cuban revolution.[6]

The cycle explained by Mesa Lago in his work is character-

5. Deutscher, Isaac. *La Revolución inconclusa*, Ediciones Era, 1967 / pp. 158-172
6. Mesa Lago, Carmelo. *Cuba en la era de Raúl Castro*, Editorial Colibrí, 2012 / pp. 25-52

by «volunteerism» (work performed under political pressure
on weekends and such, for example office workers going off
to cut sugarcane) and misbegotten economic plans centralized by the State, such as planting Caturla coffee around
Havana or the drying up of the Zapata Swamp to turn it into
arable land.

Fidel Castro gradually began to feel pressure from the Soviet
Union to substitute these extreme idealistic principles and
economic volunteerism with central planning to include
material incentives and accounting controls in financial
operations, connected to corporate efficiency, planning, and
a socialist market.

In this dynamic, Fidel Castro ended up giving in to these
political pressures from the Soviets, although always
showing traits of rebellion and of independent revolutionary
posturing.

Right from early victorious days of the revolutionary process in
1959, Fidel Castro initiated an authoritarian dynamic of
detouring the revolution towards Marxism which caused those
revolutionaries of a Social Democrat or Christian Socialist
tendencies to leave the revolutionary government or to be separated by repression, without any other options or possibilities.

This authoritarian one-man tendency in Fidel Castro,
unleashed a tough and relentless struggle to overthrow his
government, directed by non-Communist revolutionary
cadres which found the U.S. government ready to help, at
least theoretically, this varied and extensive Cuban political

opposition.

One cannot fail to mention that this distancing process of the first revolutionaries to leave the revolutionary process began with the destitution of the revolutionary President Manuel Urrutia (1959), who had defended Fidel Castro during his trial for the Moncada Barracks assault (1954) having been named president at the beginning of the revolutionary process in 1959.

These separations and conflicts inside the Cuban revolution went on after the resignation of Prime Minister José Miró Cardona (1959); the resignation and exile of the Chief of the Air Force, commander Pedro Luis Díaz Lanz (1959) and the surprise resignation and prison sentence of commander Húber Matos (1959), military chief of Camagüey Province. On the other hand, the accusations of sectarianism against the revolutionary group —March 13th Directory— for having possession of arms in the San Antonio Barracks (1959) and the public disqualification of the other guerrilla group the Second Front of Escambray (1959), both unleashed publicly by Fidel Castro, increased the existing tensions among the revolutionary groups that had fought Fulgencio Batista's dictatorship.

All these initial purges, together with the disqualification by Fidel Castro of revolutionaries having a democratic bent, gave rise to a rapid process of militarization and loyalty to the *caudillo*, the top military chief of the rebel army. All revolutionaries that rejected Fidel Castro's authoritarianism were purged, demoted and some jailed.[7] A complete process of ideological and political radicalization spread across Cuba, which will culminate, in less than two years, with the installation of a Marxist Socialist regime in the Island, and to the abandonment of democratic programs with guarantees for freedom of the press, elections in 18 months and the restoration of the 1940 Constitution, which had been the basis of the political and ideological program of the Cuban revolution, able to dethrone dictator Fulgencio Batista on December 31, 1958.

During this period, the first democratic thought organizations of revolutionaries were created to try to stop the radicalization towards Communism exhibited by Fidel Castro and company.[8]

Initially, both Fidel and Che coincided in proposing revolutionary centralism and state planning for the economy, with strong elements —from both— revolutionary and productive volunteerism. We cannot overlook the fact that these two leaders agreed on the establishment of Revolutionary Tribunals and firing squads that initially judged and shot many in the military who had been adept to the dictatorship of Fulgencio Batista, and who had not been able to escape the Island.

Later on, these tribunals continued to shoot common citi-

---

7. Suchlicki, Jaime. *Breve historia de Cuba*, Ediciones Pureplay Press,/ pp. 200-207
8. Ros, Enrique. *El clandestinaje y la lucha armada*, Ediciones Universal, 1995 / pp. 61-203

that opposed the Communist dictatorship as well as condemning the first revolutionaries who had opposed the detour taken by the Cuban regime towards Communism, such as high-ranking officers Porfirio Ramírez, Humberto Sorí Marín, Manuel Beatón, Fernando Valle Galindo and Sinesio Walsh, among many others.[9]

The implementation once again of the firing squads in the Island in 1959, set back the Cuban revolutionary process to the Colonial Era, when the Spaniards would execute many Cuban patriots, including eight medical students on November 27, 1871.

It is noteworthy that the place where more Cubans were shot to death in the early days of the revolutionary regime was in La Cabaña Fortress, an old military Spanish fort which during the Republic had become the artillery regiment of the Cuban Army. Che Guevara was the head of this unit in La Cabaña during the firing squads in those first months of 1959.

Together with this aspect of revolutionary violence, the Cuban revolution decreed the nationalization of U.S. companies established in Cuba, affecting powerful and influential US-American interests in the Island, provoking the ire of the administration of U.S. President Dwight Eisenhower, which immediately triggered a program, from the White House, to incentivize the overthrow of Fidel Castro's regime.

Fidel Castro made the decision of approaching the Soviet

---

9. Encinosa, Enrique G. Escambray, *La guerra olvidada*, Editorial SIBI, 1989 /pp. 137-165

Union, inviting Anastas Mikoyan, Vice Prime Minister of the Soviet Union to visit the Island in February 1960, in search of forging a close economic and military alliance with the Communist Soviets of the USSR. Meanwhile, Che was proceeding with his plan to industrialize Cuba, conducting mobilizations throughout the Island, all the while keeping in place the volunteer work plan, as one of the principal engines of his strategic vision for the development of the economy in the hopes of coming up with the «new man» through «volunteer» work within the revolutionary process.

In 1959, the Cuban economy began a long process of improvisation, state controls and moral incentives that disarticulated the efficient productive capitalist mechanism that had always held sway in the Island.

With the triumph of the Cuban revolution in 1959, Cuba was among the Latin American countries enjoying the most prosperous economy and being very advanced socially, on par with Argentina, Uruguay, Chile and Costa Rica.

The years and decades that followed mark the deterioration of the booming productive capacity of Cuba before 1959, due to the prevailing centralization, of the errors caused by early volunteerism, and by an irrational Statism applied to all levels of the national economy.

On the other hand, the political consolidation of the revolutionary process by Fidel Castro took hold due to the failure of the Bay of Pigs invasion, organized and directed by the U.S. Central Intelligence Agency (CIA), in addition to the defeat of anti-Castro revolutionary fronts in the mountains of

Escambray, Pinar del Río and Sierra Maestra and in the plains of Matanzas Province, due to lack of arms and munitions to fight. To all the above is added the disarticulation of the underground movement that had been operating in Cuban cities, with the goal of articulating a conspiracy network to do in the government of Fidel Castro.

The 1962 Cuban Missile Crisis between the U.S. and the USSR started with a discovery on October 15th that showed that Fidel Castro had allowed the installation of Soviet nuclear missile bases on Cuban territory, which brought into evidence that his relationship with the Union of Soviet and Socialist Republics, USSR, had consolidated to the point of aggressiveness against the United States.

Facing the U.S. maritime military quarantine ordered by President John F. Kennedy, the Soviets removed their missiles from Cuba without seeking the agreement and against the will of Fidel Castro.

This made clear that the Cuban regime lacked any authority to decide about a matter of such importance and this directly affected the sovereignty of the country. This dispute occasioned by the Soviet missiles installed in Cuba brought to light the hatred of Fidel Castro towards the United States and his lack of scruples in managing political relations with adversary states. Additionally, it revealed the degree of control that the Soviet Union held over the Cuban regime.

Within this context of the first few years of the Cuban revolutionary process, we reach the years 1964 and 1965, witness to the frequent travels of Che Guevara to the Congo, Guinea,

Egypt and China, in addition to his appearance in international conferences trying to incentivize Marxist guerrilla focal fronts in the African continent to liberate it from the colonial rule that was still in existence in most of the countries, and to negotiate with some African leaders regarding the possible participation of Cuban guerrillas in the insurrectional liberation processes existing in those places.

February 25, 1965, a date which could have gone unnoticed in the History of the Cuban Revolution, turns out to be an important pivotal point in the development of this present research, because it sped up the ideological distance — perhaps it is the beginning of the break up— between Fidel Castro and Che Guevara.[10]

On this day, Che —on his way to Algiers— expressed during the Second Economic Seminar of Afro-Asian Solidarity, during a transcendental political speech, his disagreement with the mercantilist vision held by the Soviet Union in its help to the guerrilla movements and to underdeveloped countries.

Che's denunciation not only pointed to the Soviets as being petty, but also accused them of acting in complicity with imperialist exploitation, similar to that exerted by the United States.

This public discrepancy between Che and the Soviets mani-

---

10. Lee Anderson, John. *Che Guevara*, Grove Press, NY, 1997 / pp. 546-547 / 586-588

in Algiers, while Fidel Castro proceeded with his dynamics of consolidating little by little the close collaboration with the Soviet Union, the USSR, in all possible spaces of Cuban national life, represents the inflexion point or the break up, at least ideologically and politically, between Fidel Castro and Che Guevara.

Let's read revealing fragments of the speech:

«The truths of socialism, plus the raw truths of imperialism, forged our people and showed them the path that we have now taken consciously. To advance toward their own complete liberation, the peoples of Asia and Africa must take the same path. They will follow it sooner or later, regardless of what modifying adjective their socialism may take today. For us, there is no valid definition of socialism other than the abolition of the exploitation of one human being by another. The development of the underdeveloped should cost something to the Socialist countries, alright. Additionally, one cannot trust Socialist countries that play a balancing act between Capitalism and Socialism, trying to utilize both forces as counterweight elements to extract from this competition some particular advantage. A new policy of absolute seriousness should direct relations between the two groups of societies. It is good to emphasize, once again, that the means of production should preferably be in the hands of the State, so that gradually the signs of exploitation may begin to disappear.

A conclusion must be drawn from all this: that socialist countries must help pay for the development of countries now starting out on the road to liberation. We state it this way with no intention whatsoever of blackmail or dramatization, nor are we looking for an easy way to become closer to the Afro-Asian peoples; it is rather our profound conviction.

We believe the responsibility of aiding dependent countries must be approached in such a spirit. There should be no more talk of developing mutually beneficial trade based on prices forced on the backward countries by the Law of Value and the international relations of unequal exchange that follow from the Law of Value.

How can it be «mutually beneficial» to sell at world market prices the raw materials that cost the underdeveloped countries immeasurable sweat and suffering, and to buy at world market prices the machinery produced in today's big automated factories?

The socialist countries have the moral duty to put an end to their tacit complicity with the exploiting countries of the West.

Socialism cannot exist without a change in consciousness resulting in a new fraternal attitude toward humanity, both at the individual level, within the societies where socialism is being built or has been built, and on a world scale, with regard to all peoples suffering from imperialist oppression.

Therefore, Socialist countries are interested as a vital matter, to have these breakdowns take place, and it is our international duty, the duty entrenched in the ideology that directs us, to contribute our efforts to effect this liberation as quickly and as deeply as may be possible.

The reply to the ominous attack of U.S. imperialism against Vietnam or the Congo should be to supply those sister countries with all the defense equipment they need».

From that historic moment on, it can be said that Che began to get away from Cuba and from Fidel Castro because, for him, the revolution was the priority in his life and he was in no position to subordinate it or himself to the economic or political interests of the Soviet Union.

All this discrepancy in outlook about the role of the Soviets gave way to the famous discussion upon his return from Algiers between Che, Fidel and Raúl, where the latter accused Guevara of being a Trotskyite, while Fidel didn't come to his defense.

Beginning with this discussion, Che began to distance himself from the centers of revolutionary power in Cuba. Already, both in vision and in their ways of thinking, both by Fidel as by Che, there are signs of irreconcilable differences regarding the management of the Cuban economy, the nature of the Soviet Union and the role of each of them in history.

This crisis environment led Che to decide to take other roads away from Cuba. That's when preparations were made for his revolutionary project in the Congo, as by then the project in Salta, Argentina, had already failed. Later we will see the Bolivian project crop up.

Che tries to convince the Chinese, during his several trips, to help out in the Congo, but what the Chinese want is for him to go back to Cuba to defend his ideas against the ideas of the Soviet Union.

These guerrilla projects by Che show evidence of improvisation and irresponsibility, which contradict the theoretical framework of revolutionary focal points and the structure of guerrilla wars in search of support from the masses to achieve revolutionary victory.

To this is added Che Guevara's own psychopathology, unleashed by acute asthma which impacts him from childhood provoking two evident symptoms in his personality: the first is his permanent flight towards the periphery in search of pure air; and the second his pattern of contempt and of violation of the human rights of others when they disagree with his points of view.

These two factors of his personality explain how in Che's mind he recreated the projects of guerrilla focal points in other areas in search of finding a paradise for his permanent revolution, and in other terms, his hostile and aggressive emotions towards his enemies, which explains his conduct as an intransigent and violent revolutionary.[11]

Guevara's mistake in his permanent flight to the periphery, to create a guerrilla focal point, was basically to disregard the very theoretical conditions required, which were present in the case of the Cuban revolution.

---

11. Lovett, Joan. *La curación del trauma infantil*, Editorial Pardos Ibérica, 2000

With the guerrilla project of Che in the Congo, began, within the Cuban revolution, what some authors, among them writer Luis Ortega, defined as «Guevarism,» a delirious and universal approach to make a revolution, which deviates from the Marxist Orthodoxy delineated by the Soviet Union.[12]

For Che, it was essential to have his escape formula away from the center, dominated in this case by the Soviets and by Fidel Castro, to keep alive from the center of power the flame of revolutionary struggle against imperialism, but in alliance with the Soviets.

Che continues to show passion for traveling the world, which initially meant leaving his parents, his family household, and his country, in his famous motorcycle trip with Alberto Granado.

Later, he justified it in other areas of the world with the revolution. In his revolutionary trajectory we see him leave Hilda Gadea, his first wife and mother of Hilda Guevara, and finally he leaves behind the government of Fidel Castro in search of new horizons for struggle.

This latest distancing from the government of Fidel Castro also takes him away from Aleida March, leaving her with the large responsibility of raising and educating the four children they had together.

Fidel Castro continued then to exhibit, as usual, his great

---

12. Ortega, Luis. *Yo soy el Che*, Ediciones Espuela de Plata, 2009 / pp. 294-301

love for controlling the center, power, his formula is to not give an inch. This is his real pragmatism which rejects unnecessary risks and which drives him definitively to align himself with the formulas of the Soviet Union.

For Che Guevara to flee to the periphery with a mission to write poetry and to encourage revolutionary focal point fronts meant to fulfill his mission to crush U.S. imperialism, an obligation, even an almost never-ending permanent passion in his life.

The ideas and revolutionary trajectory of Leon Trotsky lived in Che Guevara's mind, but Che lacked the organizational genius of the Russian, although both showed traits of naiveté that led them to a violent death.

3

ON THE WAY TO THE CONGO

CONVERSATION WITH GAMAL ABDEL NASSER. FIDEL MAKES PUBLIC HIS LETTER OF RESIGNATION, WHICH UPSETS CHE. HURRIED ESCAPE FROM THE CONGO.

«During these last few hours while in the Congo, I felt alone, as I had never been before, not in Cuba and not in my pilgrimage around the world. Never as today have I come to find myself so lonely in my journey.»

(*Congo Diary* written by Che in 1965 and edited and published by the government of Fidel Castro, 40 years later.)

C he disappeared from the Cuban national scene on March 22, 1965, two months after his last visit to China. His manifest with ill will against the Soviet Union, stated earlier that year in Algiers during the Second Economic Seminar of Afro-Asian Solidarity, forced him to leave Cuba. In one of the most stinging phrases from his February 24, 1965 speech at the Second Economic Seminar of Afro-Asian Solidarity Che proclaims that: «For us, there is no valid definition of socialism other than the abolition of the exploitation of one human being by another. The socialist countries must help pay for the development of countries now starting out on the road to liberation. We state it this way with no intention whatsoever of blackmail or dramatization, nor are we looking for an easy way to become closer to the Afro-Asian peoples.

How can it be "mutually beneficial" to sell at world market prices the raw materials that cost the underdeveloped countries immeasurable sweat and suffering, and to buy at world market prices the machinery produced in today's big automated factories?

«The socialist countries have the moral duty to put an end to their tacit complicity with the exploiting countries of the West. If these are the relationships, socialist countries are — in a certain way— accomplices for imperial exploitation. Socialist countries have the moral duty to liquidate their tacit complicity with the exploiting countries of the West.»

This argument from Che against the Soviet Union and other socialist countries, espoused with clarity in Algiers turned into a political leitmotif that he continued to express in most of the conclaves and private meetings in which he participated during those years.

In a book by Orlando Borrego, principal aid to Che Guevara and one of his best friends, *Che: el camino de fuego*, published by Ediciones Hombre Nuevo, Buenos Aires, 2011, this line of very critical thinking against the socio-economic guidelines of the Soviets is confirmed.

Borrego obtained all the material for his book directly from Guevara's pen, through Aleida March, during the time when Che was in hiding in Prague (1965), after the failure of the guerrilla in Congo.

Yet, more transcendental and explosive than the topic of the book written by Borrego with material from Che, is that he prophesizes the implosion of the Soviet Union –the direct descendant in modern history of the outrages of Joseph Stalin– a quarter century before the deafening collapse took place causing its disappearance from the face of the Earth as a viable formula or political institution.

«A serene study of Marxist Theory and of recent events places us as critics of the USSR. We believe the material is important, because Marxist research in the field of Economics is marching on dangerous road maps. The intransigent dogmatism of the Stalin era has been followed by a senseless pragmatism. And what is even more tragic, this doesn't only refer to the field of science; it is taking place in all aspects of life in socialist peoples, creating disturbances already enormously prejudicial, but whose final results are incalculable. The capitalist superstructure has increasingly influenced each time more and more production relationships and of conflicts provoked by the hybrid nature that NEP meant, which are being resolved today in favor of the superstructure: we are returning to capitalism.» [1]

This way of thinking by Ernesto Guevara, in the words of Orlando Borrego, his closest friend and confidant, distanced

---

1. Orlando Borrego. *Che: el camino de fuego*, Ediciones Hombre Nuevo, Buenos Aires, 2001.

him irreversibly and categorically from the Soviet Union, and therefore, indirectly from Fidel Castro.

The selection of going to Africa —leaving Cuba behind— was initially an idea of Guevara himself, in his revolutionary obsession to save the memory of Patrice Lumumba, executed in early 1961 in his struggle to gain independence for the Congo from the Belgian colonial influence and to so turn it into a revolutionary country.

But what is curious about looking for his next destination in the Congo, analyzed from all potential variants, represented really an anticipated failure with little chance of escape for the participants in this guerrilla project, by virtue of the very sensitive capitalist economic interests that were prevalent in that African country, which in addition to the tribalism present there and the Sino-Soviet confrontation going on, left little room for the development of this guerrilla project.

Cuban intelligence should have known in advance that despite all the maneuvers it made in Africa to counteract, together with the Soviets, the penetration work carried out by the People's Republic of China in that continent, the guerrilla of Guevara in the Congo was a high-risk project.[2]

Cuban shipments of arms and men to the Congo at this stage, financed by the Soviets, cared more about gaining political prestige in front of Marxist revolutionaries in the

---

2. Benemelis, Juan. Castro, *Subversión y Terrorismo en África*, Ed. S.Martín, 1988 / pp. 50- 51

African continent for Fidel Castro than to achieve real libera-tion from the colonial links existing in the continent.

Fidel Castro was trying to compensate on the one hand the vision of solidarity and revolutionary purity that Che had projected in his criticisms of the Soviet Union and of the United States while on the other hand trying to mitigate the political damage that the Missile Crisis of 1962 had caused him.

Once Guevara had broken ties with the Soviet Union, the possibilities of him remaining within the power structure of Cuba were forsaken, in the first instance by Fidel Castro, and secondly by the Soviets themselves, who wanted him far away from the Cuban scene.

Obviously, it was not easy for the Castro government to kick Guevara out of Cuba due to the international prestige that Che held. Above all, because the Cuban revolution had handed over its destiny and the main reins of power to the Soviet Union, which still held on to some of the lagging effects of Stalinism.

Che once again distanced himself from the center, from his home, from Cuba —in this case from his niche as minister in the government of the Cuban revolution— and once again heads for the periphery, to the unknown, to new revolu-tionary roadways, without discarding that revolutionary romanticism that perfectly fit his adventuresome personality.

Che again says good-bye to his family, this time as a father and not as a child, as if wanting to look out into a far-away

horizon in search of finding a dry place to cure his suffo-
cating asthma, once and for all, and to bring to life his revolutionary obsession of an inveterate Troskyite.

This time, he leaves behind Aleida, his wife, with several
children, although apparently she was sincerely in love with
him. But Che's objective was to create a guerrilla focal point
in Africa, so the household he was leaving behind was less
important and decisive in his life, as he would later confess
in person to Nasser in a dialog they held in Cairo in 1964.

But even more insensitive than his comment to the Egyptian
leader is the conversation he has with his wife Aleida March
when he counsels her to not hesitate to remarry if he doesn't
come back alive from this African journey. [3]

The objective of the guerrilla in the Congo could not have
been a better pretext to take Che out of Cuba without any
type of trauma or public scene. He left the Island happy,
because for him the mission was to rescue the revolutionary
flag of Patrice Lumumba. And of course, he needed to get
back to the periphery.

Che left a letter for his parents, which for some unknown
reason the revolutionary government of Fidel Castro never
sent to the parents. The text of the letter was known years
after his death.

---

3. Lee Anderson, John. *Che Guevara*, Grove Press, New York, 1997 / p. 591

Farewell letter from Che to his parents

April 1, 1965

Dear mom and pop:

Once again I feel under my heels the ribs of Rocinante (Don Quixote's horse) and I get back on the road with my shield on my arm. It has been almost ten years since I wrote you another farewell letter. As I remember it, I was lamenting not being a better soldier or a better doctor; the latter no longer interests me, as a soldier I'm not so bad. Nothing has changed in essence, except that I am much more aware, my Marxism is rooted and refined. I believe in armed struggle as the only solution for the peoples that are fighting to free themselves and I am consistent with my beliefs. Many will call me an adventurer, and I am, but of a different type, one that has skin in the game to demonstrate his truths.

This could be the definitive one. I don't seek it but it is within the logical calculus of probabilities. If it is so, here goes a last embrace. I have loved you a lot, although I have not been able to show my affection, I am extremely rigid in my actions and I feel that at times you didn't understand them. It was not easy to understand me, on the other hand, trust me, only, today. Now, a will that I have polished with the pleasure of an artist will sustain these flaccid legs and tired lungs. I will do it. Remember every now and then this little condotiero from the 20th century.

A kiss to Celia, Roberto, Juan Martín and Patotín, to Beatriz, to all.

A prodigal and recalcitrant son's embrace for you.

Ernesto.

Egyptian President Gamal Abdel Nasser, in a previous meeting with Che Guevara in Cairo, when the latter told him about his plans to join the Congolese guerrilla, told Che with complete frankness and with a hint of brutal irony «if he considered himself to be Tarzan, because a white man like him had nothing to do with the existing conditions in the guerrilla movement on the African continent».[4]

In this new revolutionary cycle Che arrived in Congo, Africa, with a group of Cuban guerrillas to fight the colonialism imposed, according to him, by Belgian and U.S. imperialism.

His passage as a guerrilla through the Congo was not successful in the least due to his lack of knowledge of the terrain, and to the lack of objective conditions for the preparation of logistics for the guerrilla, in terms of guns and lines of supply, and worse of all, on account of the undisciplined nature and magical mindset that he found among the Congolese fighters, predominantly more tribal than revolutionaries.

There is a very graphic phrase by Emilio Aragonés, a high-ranking Cuban officer and a great friend of Ernesto Guevara,

---

4. O'Donnell, Pacho. *Che, Editorial Debolsillo*, 2005 / pp. 340-341

when in a streak of particular openness, during a visit that he made to his friend already in Congolese territory, he tells him «Damn it Che, nobody knows what the hell we are doing here in Africa...»

The most significant part of Aragonés' statement is that it is as frank and as spontaneous as it is truthful.

While Che's rejection of the Soviets was clearly evident and public, his friendly connection with the Chinese became patently evident during his speech to the General Assembly of the United Nations on December 11, 1964 when he proposed the incorporation of the People's Republic of China of Mao Tse-Tung into the UN, while asking all free people in the world to go out to avenge the death in the Congo of its leader Patrice Lumumba at the hands of Belgian and American colonialists.

A few days after Che's arrival in the Congo, once he was already installed in his guerrilla camp, he noticed several elements of Congolese nature that heavily conspired against the guerrilla project to liberate the territory from Belgian colonialism:

First was the Congolese belief in —dawa— a magic ointment which is a mixture of herb juice to be applied on the skin achieving a hermetic seal against enemy bullets. Congolese fighters believed in it as an infallible protective element.

Second, they wanted to drink a processed corn flour or cassava flour drink —pombe— which was very popular with the fighters and which caused them to be very frequently drunk.

Third, there was generalized indiscipline among the guerrilla fighters due to the existent tribes and the lack of political indoctrination. Each tribe had its chief, a sort of monarch, who would rule on all the daily big problems of the community.

Fourth, desertion was a constant among Congolese guerrillas, because they lacked the awareness of what they were fighting for. This is explained by the scant political knowledge they possessed.

Fifth, one of the main Congolese guerrilla chiefs, commander Kabila, Che's closest ally, was always absent from the guerrilla zone attending to rebel issues in Dar-el Salam, the capital of Tanzania, or in the coastal town of Kigoma, according to what Che recounts in his Congo Diary.

These characteristics ended up contaminating even some Cuban soldiers who had been sent from the Island with little military training and who also lacked the psychological makeup to support the rigors of a war bordering on tribalism in a far-away and unknown continent, as Guevara himself recognized in his Congo Diary.

Even among the guerrillas in Rwanda, coming from the small neighboring country to the north of Tanzania who had joined the Congolese Liberation Army, the aforementioned vices and issues persisted.

Some high-ranking Congolese and Rwandan chiefs would never show up in the battle front, and worse of all, both groups were apathetic and elusive in combat, as reflected by Che's notes in his Congo Diary.

The failure of the Cuban guerrilla in the Congo left several documented instances of mixed feelings and a certain level of distrust between Fidel Castro and Ernesto Guevara, as well as between the Soviets and the Chinese, and between Fidel Castro and several African leaders such as Gamal Adbel Nasser, Sekou Touré, Joseph Mobuto and Kenneth Kuanda.[5]

In a meeting twenty years later with journalist Gianni Minná, Fidel Castro relates how he had advised Che to wait and to spend time preparing cadres before going to the Congo, which, according to documents from the time, was not a wholly true or sincere statement.

For the Congolese, as the country was semi-feudal, the differences between development and underdevelopment had a greater impact than class warfare, as established in Marxist-Leninist political theory.

In the end, African tribalism was not able to assimilate the guerrilla focal point scheme of Che Guevara, rather it rejected it, coming to terms better with Belgian and Amer-

---

5. Guevara, E. *Pasajes Guerra Revolucionaria*, Océano Sur, 2009 / pp. 56-59 / 213-231

colonialists, which explains how the Cuban guerrilla strategy in Africa quickly disintegrated.[6]

The Soviet Union itself promoted, once it had become evident that the focal point guerrilla thesis was failing in Africa, a negotiated solution going behind Che Guevara, but with the notorious agreement of Fidel Castro, and the Tanzanian, Belgian and U.S. governments calling for the removal of the Argentine commander and his Cuban guerrillas, with the simultaneous removal of Belgian mercenaries, led by Mike Hoare.

The negotiation of the Soviets with the Belgians implied the support of President Joseph Kasavubu, a U.S. ally, and one of the people responsible for an assassination attempt a few years earlier against Patrice Lumumba, the Congolese revolutionary leader.

Later on, Kasavubu was deposed in a *coup d'état* led by Joseph Mobuto (one of his generals) although both –Kasavubu and Mobuto– obtained in the negotiations the support of the Soviet Union and indirectly of Fidel Castro, to end the guerrilla project of Che Guevara in the Congo.

While this was going on in the African continent, in Havana the PURSC, United Party of the Cuban Socialist Revolution was becoming the PCC, Cuban Communist Party, under the enthusiastic leadership of the Soviet Union.

This development forced Che Guevara, from Africa, to seek

6. Benemelis, Juan. Castro, *Subversión en África*, Ed. S.Martín, 1988 / pp. 176-177

support among the leaders of the People's Republic of China to desperately try to keep alive his guerrilla project in the Congo, but he was unsuccessful.

During the opening speech of the nascent Cuban Communist Party on October 3, 1965, Fidel Castro passionately defended the Soviet Union making stinging criticisms of the People's Republic of China.

In later interviews with the newspapers *Marcha* of Uruguay and *Al Taliah* in Egypt, Che renewed his proposals of solidarity towards the recognition of the Chinese in the United Nations and began to criticize on his own terms the Soviet methods that were erroneously being applied to the Cuban economy.

There is no doubt but that Che Guevara was insistent and obsessive in his mistaken vision that in Africa the battle to overthrow imperialism would be fought, when in fact the continent was very far from exhibiting the objective conditions for that worldwide revolutionary objective.

That is why the end of this guerrilla adventure in the Congo could not have been more demoralizing for the Cuban revolutionaries, including their Argentine guerrilla chief.

Let's read some passages from the book that capture Che's sad experience in the Congo, written in Prague, which, in an incomprehensible turn of events, the Cuban government has never dared to publish verbatim

The decision to publish, forty years after it had been written by Che, a redacted and fragmented version of the Congo

Diary, is a magnificent evidence of the duplicity of Fidel Castro regarding the memory of Ernesto Guevara.

Regardless, despite the censorship exerted in the edition of the published book in 2009, reading some moments of Che's narrative about the guerrillas in the Congo, it is easy to realize the dimensions of the disaster.

This part of the diary refers to the instance when the hard decision to retreat from the Congo was made, and Che describes it as follows: «The way in which the Congolese comrades would see the evacuation seemed to me to be denigrating, our retreat was a simple escape, and worse even, we were accomplices of the deceit in which we were leaving these people on the ground. On the other hand, who was I now? I got the impression that, after my farewell letter to Fidel, the comrades began to see me as a man of other latitudes, as somewhat removed from the concrete problems of Cuba, and so I was not eager to demand the final sacrifice to stay there. That is how I spent the last hours, alone and perplexed, and in the end, at two in the morning the ships arrived with the Cuban crew that had arrived that same afternoon, and it got on the way immediately. There were too many people for the boats and the hour was late, and I set the limit for departure at three in the morning; at five thirty there would be daylight and we would be halfway into the lake. The evacuation was organized; the ill went up, then all the Chiefs of Staff of Masengo, some forty people selected by him, all the Cubans went up, and then a painful, lamentable and shameful spectacle began; I needed to reject men who were pleading to be taken onboard; there was not a single hint of greatness in this retreat, there was not one gesture of rebellion. The machine guns were at the ready and I had men ready in case that, following custom, they would try to intimidate us with an attack from land, but none of that took place, only moaning, while the chief of the escapees imprecated to the beat of the moorings as they were untied.

We navigated the length of the lake without problems despite the slowness of the boats, and in full daylight we arrived in Kigoma, sharing our arrival with the cargo ship that made the journey between Albertville and this port.

It seemed as if a mooring had split and the exultation of Cubans and Congolese spilled over like a boiling liquid over the small container of these little ships, hurting me without contaminating me; during these last few hours of my stay in the Congo I felt alone as I had never been, not in Cuba or in any part of my pilgrimage around the world. I could say more: Never did I see myself so alone again in all my journey.»

It doesn't take much to understand that Che Guevara's friendly relations with the Chinese, known by everyone, had to have had disastrous consequences for denouement of Che and his Cuban guerrillas in the Congo, due to the role that the Soviet Union ended up playing in the negotiation that abruptly took Guevara out of African territory.

If the Congolese scenario is reviewed carefully before the arrival of Guevara in that territory in 1965, we find the intervention by Belgium, the U.S., South Africa and Cuban exile airborne troops, all with the acquiescence of the UN's Operation Red Dragon included the participation of 450 Belgian soldiers from an elite airborne unit, with the U.S. guaranteeing air transportation and military intelligence by the CIA, in addition to airplanes piloted by Cuban exiles living in the United States, while the South Africans placed the city under siege.

This same year, 1965, in the middle of Che's efforts to encourage the Congolese guerrilla, Joseph Mobuto was taking over power with the support of Western countries, and even with the consent of the Soviet Union.

Keeping in mind all these adverse and complicated circumstances, we have to admit that Che Guevara was late in coming to the Congo to try to free it from colonialism. Revolutionary groups that had surged during the postcolonial era were all fleeing before the overpowering advance of the Belgians and the South Africans. At this time the confrontation between Fidel Castro and Mao Tse-Tung was red hot because of the decision by the Cuban leadership to participate in the Congress of Communist Parties (pro-Soviet) that took place in Havana and whose main objective was the expulsion of China from the international Communist sphere.

One could see that Che Guevara, since the homage that Chou-en-Lai paid him in the Great Hall of the People, (1961), was inclined to seek a close collaboration with the Chinese. Additionally, his public rift with Soviet methodology was evident.[7] This political framework in the African continent changed in a drastic way precisely from early 1965 to 1966 due to coups d'état triggered by political tribalism and to the great power influence that the Belgians and the Americans held in the continent. In Algeria, President Ben Bella, a great ally of Fidel Castro and a friend of Che Guevara, was deposed in a *coup d'état* in 1965. At that time on Algerian territory there were some 20 guerrilla training camps partially financed by Cuba with financial support from the USSR. All these camps were closed down right away after the fall of Ben Bella. A year later, Kwame Nkrumah, revolutionary President of Ghana, was overthrown by another coup inspired by the U.S. and Belgium.

During the whole period of 1965-1966 the revolutionary guerrilla movement recoiled in the Congo in the face of important cities and ports in the country falling into non-Communist hands, forcing guerrilla forces to fall back towards the north of Sudan.

In another angle of this complex and contradictory panorama, the publication and reading of the personal farewell letter from Che to Fidel, dated October 3, 1965, unleashed a strong reaction from Guevara, who didn't understand why Fidel had made it public, placing his life in danger because it made enemy foreign intelligence services know that he was leaving the Island to head for other places.

What was worse was that Che assumed, not without reason,

---

7.   Castañeda, Jorge G. *La vida en rojo*, Alfaguara, 1997 / pp. 232-233

that Fidel Castro's intention in reading his letter was to implicitly close off his possibilities of returning to Cuba as a Cuban official.

Guerrilla Daniel Alarcón Ramírez, alias «Benigno» one of Che's closest lieutenants– currently exiled in Paris and very loyal to Guevara during his whole life as a revolutionary– said that when Che found out that Fidel had read his letter during the session to announce the creation of the Communist Party in Havana, he crumpled his cap and said in indignation that «things are taking a different course, because agreements between friends are being violated, and from the shadows the cult of personality is poking, it seems that Stalin has not died».[8]

Then the deep sensation of loneliness that Che talks about in his diary when he has to leave the Congo, and hurriedly crosses Lake Tanganika fleeing towards Tanzania is manifested in his statement: «Never did I see myself so alone again in all my journey.»

But even more grave and compromising for Fidel Castro in these circumstances of the disaster in the Congo, which Che Guevara found out in great detail, was his support for the Soviet Union's attitude to negotiate a reconciliation in Africa between the two factions, calling for the exit of both the Belgian fighters as well as Che Guevara's Cuban guerrillas, at the very time when Che was preparing offensives and

---

8. Alarcón Ramírez, (Benigno): *Memoria un soldado cubano*, Tusquets, S.A.1997 / pp.116-118

ambushes against the Belgian mercenaries in the combat zone.

This shows that both the Soviets and Fidel Castro placed the Belgian warriors and the Cuban guerrillas commanded by Ernesto Guevara at the same level in the negotiation. This conspiracy between Fidel Castro and the Soviets, the Belgians, the Tanzanians and the Americans was what was more disappointing to Che Guevara in his precipitous flight from the Congo to Prague.

In these days of personal depression due to the failure in the Congo, Che got the news of the death of his mother Celia, his most beloved family member and the one emotionally closest to him, the woman that formed him and turned him into a dreamer of adventures.

When he got the devastating news of the passing of his mother, he wrote a short narrative which he called *La Piedra* or «*The Stone*,» referring to a keychain with a small stone that his grandmother had given him which he would take to the Congo, together with a silk handkerchief that his mother had given him as proof of her love.[9]

All these objects, with his pipe, his pen and the sheets to write his diary, went with him in his African adventure. Che then wrote down his wish that if he were to die, the handkerchief from his mother was to be used to close his jaws, and

---

9. Constenla, Julia, Celia, *la madre del Che*. Editorial Sudamericana, 2004 / pp. 273-278

that if he were to break his arm, then it would serve as a sling.

With this emotional collapse, Che left the Congo hurriedly crossing Lake Tanganika. This escape, of which he is able to miraculously escape alive, makes him take refuge in Prague, after spending a few days interned in the Cuban Embassy in Dar el Salam, in Tanzania.

Let's return to some excerpts found in the Congo Diary in his own handwriting, confirming the previous assessment, which occasioned this present historical work:

«This is the story of a failure. It descends from the anecdotal detail, as happens in war episodes, but is nuanced by observations and critical spirit because I believe that, if this story is to have any importance, it would be to allow us to extract experiences that may serve other revolutionary movements. More correctly, this is the story of a breakdown. When we arrived in the Congo, the Revolution was in a period of hiatus; then, several episodes took place that caused a definitive regression, at least at this time, and in that scenario is the great field of battle that is the Congo. The most important thing here is not the story of the breakdown of the Congolese Revolution, whose causes and characteristics are too deep to cover them all from my point of observation, but rather the process of the degeneration of our fighting morale, because the experience that we began cannot be wasted, and the initiative of the International Army of the Proletariat should not die after a first defeat. Among all the chiefs of the Chiefs of Staff and the so-called brigade chiefs, not one can be identified as having the conditions to be a national leader.

The chiefs of the local peasants are the kapitas and presidents; they were named by the previous Lumumba administration, or by his followers, who wish to be the germ of a civilian administration, but facing the reality of the presence of tribes, the easy road of making the chiefs of the tribes into presidents and kapitas was chosen.

There was never the necessary integration in the Congo and it cannot be blamed on skin color —so black were some that they could not be distinguished. Ours were foreigners, superior beings, and they made it obvious too frequently. The Congolese, sensitive in the extreme due to the outrages suffered in the hands of the colonialists, would notice certain gestures of contempt in the treatment from the Cubans, and I felt it very deeply.

Another barrier was language; it was difficult for a troop such as ours, immersed in a mass of Congolese to work without speaking their language. Another difficulty which we put up with, which needs to have a lot of attention paid to it in the future, is the support base.

Relatively large quantities of money disappeared into their insatiable mouths and infinitesimal quantities of food and equipment arrived for the troops on the field.

The first condition is that command has to be indisputable and absolute in the areas of operations, with rigorous controls over the support base, discounting the natural controls to be exercised from the higher echelons of the Revolution, together with the selection of men to accomplish these tasks, which should be done ahead of time.

In my reactions I was uneven; I kept up for a long time an attitude that could be called excessively compliant, and, at times, I had very cutting and very hurting outbursts, perhaps because of an innate characteristic in me; the only sector with which I maintained correct relationships without failure was with the peasants, because I am used to political language, to the direct explanations. And so I decided to not demand the greatest sacrifice in the most decisive moment. It was an inner tether, psychical. For me it was easy to stay in the Congo; from the point of view of the self-esteem of a fighter, it was the thing to do; from the point of view of my future activity, if not what was best for me, it made no difference at this time. When I was weighing the decision, it weighed on me to know how easy the decisive sacrifice would be.

Cuba doesn't retreat from its obligations nor can it accept a shameful escape leaving behind our brethren in disgrace, at the mercy of the mercenaries. We would only abandon the struggle if, on account of fundamental causes or an act of nature, or if the Congolese themselves were to request it, but we would fight for this not to happen. It is proper to call the attention of the government of Tanzania regarding the agreement reached; it is like Munich, it leaves the hands of the neocolonialists free. Against imperialism there is no room for retreat or postponement, the only language is force. If the situation of the Congo is stabilized with this government,

Tanzania will be in danger, surrounded by hostile countries to a greater or lesser intent. The revolution could subsist here without Tanzania, but at the expense of great sacrifices, and it will not be our responsibility if it is destroyed for lack of aid, etc.

It would be up to the government of Tanzania to maintain telegraph communications, to grant permission for the shipment of food at least once or twice a week, allow us to bring two fast boats, give us some of the stored armament once and permission to let couriers through every 15 days.

Mbili's letter arrived from the Lubonja front; in it he told me that the pressure on his men from the Congolese was extreme, that he didn't think that he would be able to resist any longer; low morale was prevalent. He was warning me of a conspiracy by some Cubans to ask me to retreat from the fight.»

One incontrovertible evidence of the behavior of the government of Tanzania, with the support of the USSR and the government in Havana is shown by this exchange between the letter dated November 16 by the African Rwandan commander Joseph Mundandi, addressed to Che Guevara, whose *nom de guerre* was Tatú, and the comment by the Argentine guerrilla in his diary.

«Comrade Tatú: In reference to the situation, which is very grave, I inform you that I am unable to hold my position and to guarantee its defense. The population has betrayed us, depositing its trust in enemy soldiers who are better led than us, and have good information about our position. I beg you to understand. I have decided to conduct a fighting retreat. I am not abandoning our Cuban comrades, yet I must face my responsibilities to the Rwandan people. I cannot expose all the forces of the Rwandan comrades to their possible destruction, which would not be proper by a good revolutionary commander. A revolutionary, in addition to being a Marxist, needs to analyze the situation and avoid a war of attrition. If all the comrades perish, it would be my fault; I had wanted to help that revolution to be able to do the same in my country. If the Congolese are no longer fighting, I prefer to die in our own land, the land of the Rwandan people. If we die on the way, it will also be fine.

Please receive my revolutionary sentiments,

Mundandi.»

To which Che responds pertinently in his diary:

«The departure of Rwandan fighters took place on the 18th. Tanzania, who had just blocked in its territory several arms and materiel convoys headed for the guerrilla, also faltered. Massengo also proposed to give up the fight.»

Idelphonse Massengo was the chief of the Chiefs of Staff of the Eastern Front in the Congo.

Additionally, a memorandum by the Central Intelligence Agency, written in 1965, report number 2333/65, among other things, states the following to corroborate previous statements: «Castro's wish to drive away Ernesto (Che) Guevara confirms the change in Cuban policy in the past year.»

This CIA memo states «that the separation of Guevara from power is apparently the result of his persistent opposition to the political practices recommended by the USSR.»

At this juncture, being against the Soviets, Che Guevara loses the political space he had gained in Cuba. After the disaster of the Cuban incursion in the Congolese Revolutionary War of 1965, which Che Guevara himself describes in his *Congo Diary*, as: «the story of a failure...more exactly the story of a breakdown» the Argentine guerrilla fighter had no other way out but to go in search of another peripheral zone, which in this case, inconceivably, would seem to be Bolivia.

It's worthwhile to mention that Che resisted up to mental exhaustion the acceptance of surrender which represented the abandonment of the guerrilla: «the situation is crumbling, whole troops and peasants change sides...we want to know the outcome of the report to Cuba about the Commission, to discuss it with the government of Tanzania...we plan to retreat from this place and to effect the evacuation of most of the Cubans in a second phase... a few of us will remain as a symbol of prestige for Cuba...inform Cuba...in fact the idea to stay behind kept going in my mind until late into the night, and perhaps I would not have made any decision, but rather I became one more escapee.»

Finally Che accepted defeat and left. Then he took refuge in Prague, deeply upset with Fidel Castro for having made public his farewell letter, which was a document to be read only in case of his death. To his anger, it was added the conviction that Fidel was in cahoots with the Soviet Union and with Tanzania in the complex decision to dismantle the Cuban guerrilla force in the Congo.

Che, additionally, felt emotionally collapsed from the death of his mother Celia. To this was added a greater miff; due to his sagacious intelligence, he had recognized that in reading publicly his letter of resignation Fidel was publicly closing his political return to Cuba.

It has to be kept in mind that the Congo is the second great failure of revolutionary focal point theory by Che Guevara, because in Salta, Argentina, his compatriot and friend Jorge Massetti (1963), had lost his life, together with an Argentine revolutionary group, trained in Cuba, in a failed attempt to create a guerrilla front in Argentine territory, under the direct guidance of Che Guevara.

Massetti's guerrillas, after extensive training in Cuba, received the order from Guevara to begin guerrilla warfare in Argentina. The guerrilla group set up shop in the Province of Salta, under the name People's Guerrilla Army, EGP, with support points in Bolivia, Córdoba and Buenos Aires. Jorge Massetti had the rank of Second Commander, reserving the rank of First Commander for Ernesto Guevara who would later join in. After sending a letter to the democratic Argentine President Arturo Illía announcing his decision to begin armed struggle, different complications began to befall the group, the biggest one was the lack of peasant incorporation into the guerrilla, which led to its complete collapse in 1964.

Some of the most distinguished members of the guerrilla group died in combat, such as the Cuban Hermes Peña, one of the men in Guevara's inner circle; others were arrested, while Jorge Massetti disappeared into the jungle without leaving a trace.

In this catastrophic context, at some time between March 17 and April 17, 1964, Che Guevara met secretly with Juan Domingo Perón in the house where he lived in exile in Madrid, to financially support Perón political return to Argentina, an attempt which finally didn't materialize due to the opposition of the Brazilian government that year.

Perón had pledged, by accepting aid funds from Guevara, to support Guevara's guerrilla initiative in Salta, Argentina, but as his return to Argentina was aborted, the project fell through.

The failure of the guerrilla in Salta, Argentina, made Che evaluate the possibility of participating in places other than his country, or even in other continents. This is how Africa appeared on the horizon.

Once he had left behind the traumatic experience of the disastrous Congolese guerrilla, Che once again considered Argentina as his next guerrilla destination, that is, his new path to the revolutionary periphery.

But from Havana, Fidel Castro and the General Intelligence Directorate (DGI) of the Cuban revolutionary government saw great danger in utilizing Argentina as a country for Guevara's adventures, due to the specific political weight of Argentina in the continent.

Then, the erroneous and even suspicious selection of Bolivia as the next revolutionary objective for Che Guevara appeared, keeping in mind that that Latin American country, of all others, was the one presenting the least objective conditions to achieve support from the peasants for any guerrilla process, by virtue of the fact that the nationalist revolution of Paz Estensoro in 1956 had distributed land to the workers in the fields and had guaranteed them democratic rights, such as the right to vote, something never seen before in their history.

Now a refugee in Prague, Che, emotionally devastated and sad, with the recent knowledge of the death of his mother, puts his sights again on guerrilla focal points in Argentina, refusing to go back to Cuba.

Many were the pleas and actions, among them from his wife Aleida March, for Che to quit his place of refuge and return to Cuba before setting off for a new destination. He didn't want to go back to the Island under any circumstance, even for a short training period. His emotional and political distancing from Fidel Castro, for the protectionist umbrella of the Soviet Union over Cuba, and his critical opinion of the Soviets, was a discrepancy that at the time seemed insurmountable.

From Prague, Che wrote a letter in 1965 to his friend Armando Hart, where he harshly criticized the Cuban «ideological continuism» with respect to Soviet manuals for the teaching of Marxism, a point of view he shared with the journal *Pensamiento Crítico*, (*Critical Thinking*) published in

Havana by recognized academics such as Fernando Martínez Heredia and Aurelio Alonso, among others, all from the Philosophy Department of the University of Havana. While this group of professors were exhibiting an anti-Soviet tilt, Fidel continued to close political ranks with the Soviet Union without publicly contradicting his solidarity for the international proletariat and worldwide liberation movements.

Finally, after multiple pleas from Aleida March and Ramiro Valdés, both are able to convince Guevara of the benefit of a clandestine stay in Cuba to recover from his deteriorated health and to prepare for the new revolutionary destination, which would be Bolivia.

Guevara's return to Havana on July 21, 1966 takes place in secrecy, after spending four months at the Cuban Embassy in Dar el Salaam and several additional months in Prague. From the time of his return to Cuba from Prague, a bois-terous meeting is known to have taken place between Fidel and Raúl, regarding discrepancies over the route of the Cuban revolution led by the hand of the Soviet Union, and Che's complaint to Fidel for having published his farewell letter.

Some who were with Che during his preparatory stay in Cuba, such as guerrilla fighter Benigno, considers that the death of his mother Celia, the failure of the guerrilla in the Congo, and previous to that the disaster of Massetti's guer-rillas in Salta, Argentina, together with his public discrepan-cies regarding the road taken by the Cuban revolution in submitting to Soviet control, had hit hard at Che Guevara's emotional psyche regarding his lack of trust in the leadership of Fidel Castro.

In these circumstances, Che lived with the emotional need to erase from his mind all the mishaps of the disastrous Congolese revolution, leaving behind his differences with Fidel Castro for his dependency with the Soviet Union to prepare for his next destination, which Che would have preferred to be Argentina and/or Perú, but that Fidel and his staff at the Central Intelligence Department (CI) decided would be Bolivia.

At this time it is known that the Soviet intelligence service KGB and the U.S. one, the CIA, knew that Che had participated in the failed guerrilla attempt with the Liberation Front in the Congo, and that possibly he would be in search of his next destination or guerrilla focal point for his revolutionary objectives.

Che's most strongly felt desire —during his stay in Prague— was to depart from his exile towards Argentina, to continue his guerrilla activities in his native country, but as we already know, the Cuban leadership in Havana vehemently opposed that destination strongly blocking it.

Four months would Che stay in Cuba, and by November 2, 1966 he left the Island headed for his new destination, Bolivia.

By the middle of that year he had sent an advanced party of two of his right-hand men, Harry Villegas, alias Pombo and

Carlos Coello, alias Tuma, to join José María Martínez Tamayo, alias Papi, who were already on the ground in Bolivia organizing and evaluating the guerrilla situation. On November 3, 1966, Che Guevara arrived in La Paz, Bolivia, under the identity of Adolfo Mena, an Uruguayan economist. The last stage of his biological life as revolutionary was beginning, filled with contradictions and avatars of doubtful credibility.

4

BOLIVIA, A MISBEGOTTEN OBJECTIVE

THE ONLY COUNTRY IN LATIN AMERICA WHERE PEASANTS WERE THE OWNERS OF MOST OF THE LAND. MONJE, THE COMMUNIST THAT BETRAYED CHE IN BOLIVIA

«Total lack of contact with Manila (Fidel), La Paz and Joaquín, which brings us down to 25 men making up the group.»

(Che's Bolivia Diary, May 1965)

Authors who have researched the development of the guerrilla focal point that cost Che his life in Bolivia find, to their surprise, that Guevara's true wish for that revolutionary effort was not the Bolivian plateau but rather his native land of Argentina, or if it were not possible, then Perú.

Bolivia became a third alternative since both the General Intelligence Directorate (DGI) and Fidel Castro rejected the two first options, as we mentioned in the previous chapter.

The government of Havana lived those first few years of revolutionary triumph in 1959 with the obsession —more emotional than rational— to start guerrilla fronts in Latin America, with the objective of repeating the actions of the Sierra Maestra and to politically strike at the government of the United States and enemy governments ruling in the Latin American continent.

From Havana, attempts were made to open guerrilla fronts in Nicaragua, El Salvador, Guatemala, Venezuela, Perú, Argentina, Colombia, and finally Bolivia. However, despite his recognized public strategic discrepancy with the Soviet Union, Che Guevara, given his emotional need to go far from Cuba and to search for a country in which to create a guerrilla focal point, accepted to have Bolivia as his next destination, with the fragile and doubtful alliance of the Bolivian Communist Party, which Fidel Castro and the the Cuban Intelligence Department (CID), prepared and recommended.

It seems inconceivable that both Fidel Castro and Manuel Piñeiro, the chief officer of the CID, would have forgotten so quickly the meeting in Havana with Mario Monje, president of the Bolivian Communist Party in 1963, accompanied by Hilario Clauré, a member of the Politburo of that party, where the two Bolivians ratified their political position against armed struggle in their country.

In that meeting with them, facing the categorical opinion of the Bolivians, Fidel Castro then asked Mario Monje for help only for the guerrilla of the group of Héctor Béjar in Perú,

using their border areas, but without meddling in the
internal problems of Bolivia.

It is then that Fidel says in his own words to Monje: «I'm very
sorry for you guys, for Bolivia, because it is a difficult country
to wage guerrilla war in. You are a landlocked country, there
has been an agrarian reform; and so your destiny is to offer
solidarity to the revolutionary movements in other countries,
because one of the last countries that will achieve their liberation will be Bolivia. Guerrilla struggle is not possible in
Bolivia.»

These exact words from Fidel Castro in 1963 practically eliminate Bolivia, at least theoretically, from future guerrilla
activity. Mario Monje returned to Havana a few months later
and had a meeting with Che, in which he repeated the same
thing Fidel had said, something Che knew first hand from
his visit to Bolivia during his trips throughout Latin America
aboard a motorcycle with his friend Alberto Granados.

Let's also read Che's words: «I was in Bolivia, I know Bolivia
and it is very difficult to do guerrilla fighting in Bolivia. There
have been reforms, and I don't think those indigenous people
are going to join the guerrilla struggle.»

To these opinions held by the highest-ranking leaders of the
Cuban revolution —including Che's, over the negative conditions in Bolivia for a guerrilla theater of operations —one
must add the thinking of the highest-ranking leaders of the
USSR, the Union of Soviet and Socialist Republics, who
considered it counterproductive and even dangerous for the
Bolivian Communist Party to move away from the line of

peaceful coexistence held by Moscow. All these tensions between the position of the Soviet Union in cahoots with Bolivian Communists, and the final decision taken by Fidel Castro and Cuba's Central Intelligence Department –once Argentina and Perú had been discarded as areas for guerrilla warfare– that it would be Bolivia where the next Che Guevara guerrilla would happen in Latin America, open a paradoxical question mark that forces us to consider how incomprehensible it was to decide to place the guerrillas in Bolivia.[1]

One has to add that one of the most powerful elements to discard Argentina as a guerrilla theater was that the Argentine Communist Party itself, led by Victorio Codovilla, having an excellent relationship with the USSR, considered Che Guevara a Trostskyite adventurer.

Feder Burlanski, one of the closest advisors of Nikita Kruschev, the then Prime Minister of the Soviet Union, once said: «we disliked Che's position, because it served as a model for adventurers who could have caused a confrontation between the USSR and the U.S.»

This political framework to develop and push for a Cuban guerrilla, headed by Che Guevara in Bolivia, brings to mind three previous inescapable fundamental considerations:

The first is that Che, on account of his public and notorious anti-Soviet stance didn't fit in Cuba, which was speedily becoming embedded within the sphere of the Soviet Union,

---

1. Villegas, Harry. *Pombo, hombre de la guerrilla del Che*, Spanish Edit. 1995.

in the context of the Cold War, despite the contradictions and internal conspiracies that the dynamics of this relationship engendered in those years.

The second is that despite what Fidel was proclaiming in revolutionary gatherings and in the Second Declaration of Havana (1963) regarding the inevitability of revolution in Latin America, his commitments to the Soviet Union, under way or being consolidated, tended to trump the at-times incendiary rhetoric of his public speeches.

The third is that Che's appearances in different international conferences and his strong criticism of the Soviet Union, since his visit to Algiers, had granted Che Guevara's image in front of the revolutionaries of the world with a political dimension and international reach of such an extent that it was hardly acceptable given Fidel Castro's authoritarian style and absolute domination.

In January 1964, Fidel Castro visited the Soviet Union making his allegiance to the Soviets and to peaceful coexistence a matter of the public record, while for Che Guevara this policy was always wrong and despicable for its complacency with the interests of the United States.

In early 1965, Che's guerrilla campaign began in the Congo, which we already discussed in the previous chapter, ending up with a disappointing defeat, according to the Argentine guerrilla himself, which he was never able to get over emotionally speaking, as the precipitous flight crossing Lake Tanganika was something he considered an act of personal cowardice.

Once his depressing and solitary exile hiding place in Prague was over, in the company of his closest lieutenants from the Congo guerrilla war, Che reluctantly returned to Cuba to train for his final destination, which would be Bolivia.

Che Guevara took advantage of his stay in Prague to write his explosive book *Congo Diary*, which, as we stated before, was only published decades later by the government of Havana, heavily redacted.

All close eyewitness reports seem to confirm Fidel Castro's obsession with having Che Guevara return to Havana, basically so that his *Congo Diary* would not be published without his previous and exhaustive review, due to its criticism over the decision of the Cuban revolutionary government, shared by the governments of Tanzania, Belgium, the USSR and the United States, to deactivate Che's guerrilla in that area.

Finally, in the middle of this environment of lies, half-truths and recriminations between Cuban and Bolivian leaders, Che accepted to go to Bolivia, although Fidel Castro never told him about how reluctant the Bolivian Communist Party was to enthusiastically collaborate with this revolutionary project.

The evidence points to the fact that Che's plans in Bolivia were drawn up by Fidel Castro, although Che had the option to select the guerrilla fighters that would go in with him. This is in addition to the great political pressure exerted by the Soviet Union to have Che out of Cuba.

Needless to say, Fidel Castro's controlling and pragmatic mind also bubbled with the possibility that if the guerrillas were able to grow roots and were successful, then he would hold an additional card with which to pressure the U.S. and the USSR.

At the same time, the Communist Bolivians had once again decided, in mutual agreement with their Soviet comrades, to take the path of legality, of ballots, and to therefore distance themselves from the revolutionary focal point that Che wished to develop in Bolivia.

In the long term, the Soviet thesis of electoral coexistence proved to be more efficacious and realistic that armed struggle in Latin America, which was more than proven with the later electoral triumphs by Hugo Chávez in Venezuela (1999), Evo Morales (2005) in the very same Bolivia, and Rafael Correa (2007) in Ecuador. All experts on Bolivian politics coincide in pointing out that Bolivia didn't offer the best possibilities for the incorporation of the peasants in any guerrilla effort.

Ernesto Guevara knew this perfectly well, and he had proven it to his satisfaction personally on his Latin American trips, before becoming the audacious and untiring revolutionary guerrilla.

On August 2, 1953, the then president, Víctor Paz Estensoro signed in Ucureña, Bolivia, the Agrarian Reform Act, whose slogan was «land for he who tills it.» This law made it possible for two millions peasants to be incorporated as owners of their land, eliminating servitude and exploitation by owners of large estates in Bolivia.

The more than two million indigenous peasants that benefited from the Agrarian Reform of Paz Estensoro organized themselves into peasant agrarian unions and a militia to defend the Agrarian Revolution that had been passed by the Bolivian national government.

To this negative situation for guerrilla focal point development is added the strange and suspicious contradiction that Manila (Fidel Castro) would have counted on the supposed incorporation and collaboration of the Bolivian Communist Party, which was never in fact contemplated or guaranteed.

The hesitant and pro-Soviet attitude of Mario Monje, Secretary General of the Bolivian Communist Party, offered few guarantees that the Bolivian Communists would really join Che Guevara's revolutionary project and the Cuban guerrillas that accompanied him.

Monje couldn't accept that a foreigner like Che, no matter how famous, would come to direct the revolution in Bolivian territory, and he would tell his cadres in the Communist Party.

In view of the negative attitude of the Bolivian Communist Party, there was scant likelihood that Che Guevara's guerrilla project would develop in Bolivia.[2]

---

2. Mario Monje: *Carta al Comité Central del Partido Comunista Bolivia*, La Paz, July 15, 1968.

Finally, Che departs for Bolivia, and so he says goodbye to his children:

«My dear Aliusha, Camilo, Celita and Tatico (Ernesto): I'm writing from very far away and in a great hurry, so I will not be able to tell you about new adventures. It's a shame because they are interesting, and Pepe, El Caimán, has introduced me to many friends. I'll do it another time.

Now I wanted to tell you that I love you very much and that I remember you all the time, together with mama, although, you, the youngest one, I barely know you from photographs because you were very little when I left. Soon I will have a picture taken so you can see how I look now; a bit older and uglier.

This letter will get to you when Aliusha turns six, so it will serve to congratulate her and to wish her a happy birthday: Aliusha, you need to study hard and you need to help your mom in every way. Remember that you are the oldest.

You, Camilo, need to say less dirty words that cannot be said in school, and you need to get used to using them where they are allowed. Celita, always help your dear grandma with house chores and continue being so charming as when we said good-bye, remember? I bet you don't. Tatico, you grow up and become a man, then we will see what happens. If there is still imperialism we will go out and fight it. If that is done with, then you, Camilo and I will go to the moon on vacation.

Give a kiss from me to the grandparents, to Myriam and her maid, to Estela and Carmita and to all of you I send a kiss the size of an elephant, from Papa.

To Hildita, another kiss the size of an elephant, and tell her that I will soon write to her, now, I have no time left.

Papá».

Once the Cuban guerrilla had set up camp in the mountainous slopes of the Ñancahuazú River or Gold River, in indigenous nomenclature, Che writes in his field diary on November 7, 1966, the following almost providential phrase:

«Today a new stage begins. We arrived at the farm at night. The trip was good enough after arriving, conveniently through Cochabamba».

From the geographical point of view the area selected was awful for the guerrilla objective, because it was uninhabited and was far away from the border with Perú, keeping in mind that Che had always wanted the guerrilla camp to be near the Perúvian border, since this would make it easier to cross borders to gain the cooperation of the revolutionary movement in that country.

The farm selected for Che Guevara had a house with a zinc roof, which the neighbors therefore called «*la Casa de Calamina*» or «the House of Calamine». From the start of his arrival in Ñanchaguazú, Che, presaging a betrayal or ambush, decided to establish his personal camp more than half a mile away from that house.

Like a hex announcing bad news from the earliest days –
which were used by the guerrilla to organize the camp and to
reconnoiter the land in search of areas to be used as depots
and to establish a rearguard hospital– two of the most experienced Cuban guerrillas, Alberto Fernández Montes de Oca,
alias Pachungo and Harry Antonio Villegas Tamayo, alias
Pombo, who had been already in Ñancahuazú, were found
out by an employee of the farm next to Calamine House.[3]

This incident greatly disturbed Che Guevara, as it showed
that the two guerrillas were not rigorously following the
security codes required for the tasks of setting up bases for
the guerrilla project.

And so Che writes in his Bolivia Diary on November 10:
«Pachungo and Pombo went to scout with one of the Bolivian
comrades. While coming back they began to hang around
the house and the driver of the Algarañaz, who was coming
to bring the men some supplies, saw them. I really let them
have it, and we decided to move into the bush the following
day.»

In less than two weeks the Cuban guerrillas Antonio
Sánchez Díaz, alias Pinares, Eliseo Reyes, alias Rolando,
Rodolfo Saldaña, alias Rodolfo arrived at the house together
with several dissident cadres from the Bolivian Communist
Party who joined the project.

And so, gradually, others came to join up the guerrillas in

---

3.   Fernández Montes de Oca. *Diario de Pacho*. Edit. Punto y Coma, 1987 / pp.
6-7 / 97 - 99

Ñancahuazú, such as Bolivian Inti Peredo, other Bolivian cadres and the rest of the Cubans. The first designations of responsibilities by Che Guevara were assigned as follows: Vitalio Acuña Nuñez, alias Joaquín, second military chief; Gustavo Machín, alias Alejandro, chief of operations; Harry Villegas, alias Pombo, chief of services, and Dr. Octavio de la Concepción, alias el Moro or Morogoro, chief of medical services.

But all the expectations of Che's guerrillas during these first few weeks were focused on the meeting, announced on a message from Havana by Manila (Fidel Castro) to Che, confirming the meeting with Mario Monje.

In his analysis for the month of December in his diary, Che writes: «All has gone fairly well, my arrival went off without a glitch: the plans are to wait for the rest of the guys, to increase the number of Bolivians to at least 20, and to begin to operate. We are still waiting to find out Monje's reaction and how Guevara's people behave.»

This mention of another Guevara in his diary refers to Moisés Guevara, a pro-Chinese Bolivian Maoist, who Che accepted initially with the aim of stimulating Bolivian incorporation into the guerrilla group, foreseeing that Bolivians from the Communist Party would not demonstrate the required enthusiasm.

Several weeks before the awaited meeting between Mario Monje and Che Guevara, towards the end of November 1966, Regis Debray, a French journalist and writer arrived in Bolivia to join the Cuban guerrilla, being sent directly by

Fidel Castro. It was his third trip to Bolivia, as evidenced by records from his previous trips.

The arrival of Debray in La Paz, Bolivia, had the intention of letting the French writer look over the geographical area and to file a report about the best conditions for Che's guerrilla project and for his forward and rear encampments.

At this point a new question comes up for some researchers of this stage in the life of Che Guevara: how can it be understood that the intellectual Regis Debray, who was not familiar with Cuban idiosyncracy, or with Bolivian geography, and who lacked guerrilla experience, would be sent to Bolivia for such a logistical task by the Cuban government?

Years later Regis Debray himself declared, among other very negative observations about the guerrilla project in Bolivian territory and the authoritarian way of governing exercised by Fidel Castro, that Che Guevara didn't go to Bolivia to win, but to lose.»[4]

But the presence of Regis Debray in Bolivia produced another immediate negative effect, almost a boomerang reaction, because the French writer was a renowned intellectual of Maoist tendencies, which in addition to Che's anti-Soviet ideas due to his supposed Trotskyite and pro-China tilt, worsened suspicions and perceptions in the Bolivian Communist Party on a project that all seemed to indicate was closer to the influence of the Chinese and their leader Chou-en-Lai than to the Soviets and their leaders in the Kremlin.

---

4. Debray, Regis. *Praised Be Our Lords*, Editions Gallimard, 1996./ pp. 101-110

In the midst of this stressful environment between the Bolivian Communist Party and the presence of Cuban guerrillas in Bolivia under the leadership of Che Guevara, the much-awaited meeting between Che Guevara and Mario Monje took place.

On December 31, 1966, after several delays due to errors in the dates for Monje's travels to Ñancahuazú, both leaders sat down to chat.

But soon after the meeting started between both leaders insurmountable discrepancies arose because Che Guevara was not about to relinquish his military leadership over the Bolivian guerrilla to the Bolivian Communist Mario Monje.

For his part, Mario Monje and his Bolivian Communist Party could not conceive of a revolutionary operation in Bolivia commanded by a foreigner, be he Argentine or Cuban.

The breakup between Guevara and Monje took place, which places the guerrilla project in great jeopardy, because Mario Monje, the Secretary General of the Bolivian Communist Party left Ñancahuazú extremely angry at Che Guevara's obstinacy.

After the total disagreement between Monje and Guevara, it became crystal clear that such basic and preliminary matters as this coordinating meeting between the two leaders should have been discussed prior to mobilizing guerrilla fighters from Cuba and Bolivia.

But it wasn't done and in his diary, Che wrote on January 1, 1967: «Monje told me he was leaving. He left with the look of someone on the way to the gallows. My impression is that when he found out from Coco my decision to not yield on strategic matters, he held on to that point to force the rupture, since his arguments are inconsistent. In the afternoon I met with everyone and I explained Monje's attitude, announcing that we would unite with all who wished to make revolution and that I could foresee difficult moments and days of moral anguish for the Bolivians». From then on, the Bolivian Communist Party, which at the time wasn't sympathetic to armed struggle, but which had reluctantly accepted collaboration with the project at the insistence and at the prestige of Fidel Castro, would now oppose guerrilla actions in Bolivia with all its might.

Only a small group of dissident militants from the Bolivian Communist Party would go on to join Che's guerrilla force in Bolivia. In this group were, among others, Rodolfo Saldaña, Jorge Vazquez Viaña, alias El Loro, Julio Luis Méndez Korne, alias El Ñato and brothers Coco and Inti Peredo.

A few days after the disagreement or breakup between Che Guevara and Mario Monje in Ñancahuazú, the Central Committee of the Communist Party wrote a letter to Fidel Castro closing the door on cooperation with the guerrilla project headed up by Che Guevara.

The behavior of the Bolivian Communist Party was directed —from the moment of the breakup— to block and boycott any support to the Cuban guerrillas in Ñancahuazú. Facing this grave and desolate situation of having broken with the Bolivian Communist, Che reactivated his contacts with the

Bolivian Maoist leader Moisés Guevara and his revolutionary group, all of them leaders of the Bolivian Communist Party and all sympathizers of the Chinese Communist Party.

Che wrote down in his field diary —in his summary for the month of January— about the serious breakdown with Mario Monje stating the following: «as expected, Monje's attitude was evasive from the start and treacherous in the end. By now the party is arming up against us and I don't know where it will end up.»

Therefore, Che already considered the attitude of the principal leader of the Bolivian Communist Party to be treason. Then Che Guevara goes on, referring to the Bolivian Maoist leader Moisés Guevara: «up to now he has responded well. We shall see how he and his people behave in the future...Of all that we had planned, what has gone on most slowly is the recruitment of Bolivian fighters.»

These adjustments in search of recruiting Bolivians for the Cuban guerrilla in Bolivia provoked an increase in the confrontation between Che Guevara and the Communist Party of Bolivia and the majority of Communist parties in Latin America, which in general disapproved the strategy of armed struggle, being faithful to the guidelines of peaceful coexistence coming down from the USSR, the Union of Soviet and Socialist Republics.

What was inconceivable during these early days of the guerrilla process in Bolivia, which supposedly was counting on the official aid of the government of Cuba, is that Fidel Castro and his Central Intelligence Department didn't tell

Che Guevara about the letter from the Bolivian Communist Party and from Mario Monje, addressed to Fidel, where they ratify that they were cutting ties completely with the Cuban guerrilla project in Bolivia, among other additional reasons, aside from the issue of military command, due to the presence of Regis Debray in Che's guerrilla.

But worse still than all of the above —also with many confusing implications— is that Fidel Castro didn't order the immediate dismantling of the Cuban guerrilla in Bolivia, knowing perfectly well that the Bolivian Communist Party would inform the Soviet Intelligence Agency (KGB) of the presence of Guevara in Bolivia, and that that agency would do all it could to avoid the growth of the Che Guevara's guerrilla in Bolivia, as in fact happened.

There is even a frank commentary from Che after his ill-fated meeting with Monje related by Benigno in his book which goes as follows: «This ended before it began. There's nothing to do here.»

At this time, it was when Che Guevara, in his own words, gave the option to his men, Cubans or Bolivians, to have the possibility of abandoning the guerrilla, if they so wished.

A dark and fatal presentiment loomed over the guerilla project in Bolivia due to the mishap between Guevara and Monje, and for the logical implications that flow from it.

To all of this is added that in those months Fidel continued to enhance his strategy to try to improve the relations of the Cuban government with the Soviet Union, in search of strengthening his military structure, which apparently was the main reason for Che Guevara's distancing from the Cuban Revolution and Fidel Castro.

We need to add that Fidel Castro himself, during the First Tricontinental Conference in Havana issued a severe criticism of the Chinese government for having reduced Cuba's rice quota.

As a historical aside, it was at this Tricontinental meeting in January 1966 in Havana where Che Guevara announced in a taped communications the need to conquer the freedom and independence of the peoples, creating «one, two, three, four Vietnams».

Paradoxically, and even compromising, from the month of March, the initial stage, one of consolidation of the Cuban guerrilla in the Bolivian mountains, the Central Intelligence Agency, CIA, designated Robert (Papi) Shelton, as chief of the U.S. mission in Bolivia to secure U.S. military support for his fight against the guerrilla insurgency.

For his part, Fidel Castro ordered the departure from La Paz of the high-ranking Cuban Security officer Renán Montero, a very well-connected cadre in Bolivian society, who additionally was the official liaison of the Cuban government with Che Guevara.[5]

It's worthwhile to delve deeper into an almost unheard of event. This high-ranking officer of the Cuban State Security,

---

5. O'Donnelll, Pacho. *Che*, Editorial Debolsillo, 2005./ pp. 502–503

Renán Montero, alias Iván, had been planted in La Paz long ago, with the cover of being a businessman, and he had even had a romantic liaison and married a Bolivian woman, having created a network of relationships with the political power base in Bolivia.

For the Cuban guerrilla in Bolivia, this link was vital having a fundamental strategic importance. That is why it is so strange that in this initial phase of the guerrilla, now complicated by the Monje-Guevara disagreement, Montero would get the order from the Cuban government to leave Bolivia on his way to Paris, for a supposed passport or health issue.

Later, Renán Montero reappeared in Nicaragua, with the same rank as a high official in Cuban intelligence, but now linked to the Sandinista Liberation Front.

In the case of Montero, many ask: what could explain that Fidel Castro would order the departure of this high-ranking Cuban officer, the liaison between Che Guevara in the mountains and La Paz right in the middle of the formation and development of the guerrilla?

A difficult question arises, which up to now, more than fifty years later, still remains unanswered, despite all the reverences that are done in the official Cuba to the memory of Ernesto Guevara and the painstaking attention given to the family members of the Argentine guerrilla who live in the Island.

Writer Norberto Fuentes, in his biography of Fidel Castro, states, with his usual irony and acuity, that the intention of the Cuban government towards Guevara with the Bolivian guerrilla was to liquidate Che.[6]

In late 1966, the Secretary General of the Soviet Communist Party, Leonid Brezhnev, had already manifested his indignation at the presence of Che Guevara in Bolivia.

Additionally, some months later, Brezhnev reaffirmed «that the guerrilla activities in Bolivia were damaging to the true interests of the Communist cause.»

To all of this is added that in June 1967, Soviet Premier Alexei Kosigyn asked Fidel Castro to suspend his aid to all guerrilla movements in Latin America, including Che's guerrillas in Bolivia, so as not to hinder diplomatic relations between the USSR and the U.S.[7]

Quite a petition from the top Soviet leadership at a time when Che Guevara was risking his life in the guerrilla front in Bolivia!

It seems evident that the road of the Cuban guerrilla in Bolivia, plagued with errors, betrayals, desertions and erratic combat actions, very poorly designed, not discounting the gravity that the lack of peasant recruitment meant, showed that the project was by then a complicated scenario without a chance to end well for Che Guevara.

One of the first decisions by Che, once he had separated from Monje and the Bolivian Communist Party, was to

---

6. Fuentes, Norberto. *The Autobiography of Fidel*, Norton Paperback, 2010.
7. Castañeda, Jorge G. *La vida en rojo*, Alfaguara, 1997 / pp. 469 - 470

conduct a walk-through around the mountainous area surrounding Ñancahuazú. This trek, originally planned for fifteen days with the simple objective of conducting training and to *reconnoiter* the area, which is full of mountain canyons, cliffs, a few rivers, and scant edible animals, became a long, desolate and oppressive march lasting almost two months for the members of the guerrilla, by virtue of the groups lacking experienced guides that new the ins and outs of the area and the inward way of the natives of the area.

In this journey two Bolivian recruits drowned due to rains that flooded the rivers, and so the troop was forced to kill a horse for food, and the lack of water affected all of them.

Almost all historians of Che's guerrilla point to the date of March 20 as the return to camp of the troops. And it is around that date that two guerrillas from the Bolivian Maoist group of Moisés Guevara deserted the guerrilla and were detained, allowing the Security Forces of Bolivia and even the Bolivian Army to know about the Cuban guerrillas headed by Ernesto Guevara, who were found to be in Bolivia.

In the month of March, now without the backing of Renán Montero, the Cuban official liaison from La Paz, the guerrilla began to show signs of demoralization due to the rejection by area peasants to join the guerrilla. During those days French writer, Regis Debray and Argentine painter Ciro Bustos were arrested in the Bolivian mountains.[8]

---

8. Lee Anderson, John. *Che Guevara*, Grove Press, New York, 1997./ pp. 661-669

According to very accurate testimony, it seems that the betrayal of painter Bustos, who painted portraits of some guerrillas and provided detailed information about them, gave Bolivian Army Intelligence and the CIA the confirmation they needed regarding the presence of Guevara and the Cuban guerrillas in the area of Ñancahuazú.

In his summary for the month of March, Che pointed out in his field diary: «Stage of consolidation and screening of the guerrilla completed fully, slow stage of development with the incorporation of several elements arriving from Cuba, which don't look bad, and the ones from Moisés Guevara which turned out to be of a very poor level in general (2 deserters, 1 «talking» prisoner, 3 who gave up, 2 softies).»

With this very confusing political panorama, so full of recriminations among Bolivian Communists, Che had few probabilities to survive his guerrilla project in Bolivia.

As we continued to work on our investigation, the question of why Fidel Castro and his government didn't exert the greatest possible effort from Havana to reestablish contact with Che, or on the contrary to get Che out of his Bolivian predicament, cancelling his guerrilla operation, became more pressing.

To continue Che's guerrilla operation in Bolivia, without the support of the Bolivian Communist Party and without the presence of Renán Montero in La Paz, or any other designated liaison, was an almost a crazy policy with hints of being suicidal.

But the operation continued, and when the month of May arrived, Che reaffirmed in his diary: «**total lack of contact with Manila (Fidel).**»

In the month of June, Che emphasizes that «the total lack of contact with Manila continues, and peasant participation is also missing.»

The same thing happened again in July with the refrain: «lack of contact continues. The lack of peasant participation is still continuing».

In a dramatic show of how things kept on getting complicated for Che, he affirms in the month of August in his diary, «We continue without contact of any sort, fighting morale and our revolutionary legend is decreasing.»

Let's keep in mind that we are relating what Che plainly stated in his field diary, without any adjectives or stress of any kind on our part, which adds value and certainty to the human and political abandonment to which the Argentine guerrilla was submitted due to the lack of interest that the the General Intelligence Directorate (DGI) from Havana showed.

In the month of September, Che wrote in his diary, «Miguel, Coco, Julio fell, we are still without contact. The army shows more effectiveness. Important task, contact with La Paz».

For Che it was imperative in this month of September, facing constant aggressive harassment from the Bolivian Army, as his survival was at stake, to be able to re-establish contact with La Paz, the capital of the country, or with his supposed primary base of support, which was the Cuban government.

Meanwhile, some Latin American Communist parties, such as the Chilean, publicly criticized Che Guevara for his irresponsible guerrilla attitude.[9]

Symptomatic, and with signs of a strategic disaster, is the fact that since the month of March the liaison with the Cuban government in La Paz, officer Renán Montero, had been interrupted by the express order of Fidel Castro and the the General Intelligence Directorate (DGI), and what is even more revealing is that this contact was never replaced, without even a minimal effort from the government in Havana.

That is why Che insists in his diary about the importance of reestablishing those contacts with the capital of Bolivia, keeping in mind that the Bolivian Army was on his tail and that of his guerrilla force.

By the month of September Che's guerrilla was practically abandoned, lacking basic supplies and without medicine to fight his asthma.

From Havana, the Cuban government didn't move a finger nor did it try to get closer to the drama that the Cuban guerrillas were living with Che in Bolivia.

_____

9. Guevara, Ernesto: *El Diario del Che en Bolivia*, Siglo XXI Editores, 1968. / pp. 212 - 232

5

CAPTURE AND ASSASSINATION
OF CHE

HUNGRY, THIRSTY, LACKING MEDICINES FOR
ASTHMA, AND SHOELESS.

«I'm worth more alive than dead.» The Communist powers
that were in Bolivia and Havana abandoned him. «I'm
human rot, and the incident with the little mare proves that
at times I have lost it...»

(*Che's Bolivia Diary*, August 8, 1967)

From youth, a teenage Ernesto Guevara had the
tendency to like poetry —which is ironic since he
concludes his life as a revolutionary adventurer
filled with harshness, hate for his adversaries and fierce
struggles against the United States and everywhere, writing
intimate poems that reveal at least a metaphoric and literary
nostalgia within him.

These verses become, definitively, intimate objects, in search
of emotionally balancing the exigencies of his failed harsh

life as a guerrilla and revolutionary, due to his experiences in Salta, the Congo and Bolivia.

One of his more stinging poems, which he dedicated to his wife Aleida March, and another one in which he rewrites a painful and beautiful poem by poet León Felipe, a few hours and days before his death, are incontrovertible proof of the anguish that already dwelled in his inner being.

In his last hours of life, poetry became a balm to alleviate his pain and to externalize his most intimate frustrations.

The poem —dedicated to his wife Aleida March— uncovers the desolation in his soul at the time when his life approaches the end of his revolutionary struggles. These verses reflect the great doubts that lash at his soul due to the distressing conditions of hunger, thirst, rags tied around his feet and the lack of medicines that prick him cruelly during the last hours of his life:

He entitled his poem to Aledia «*Contra viento y marea*» *(Against wind and tide* or *Against All Odds)*

«This poem (*Against wind and tide* or *Against All Odds*)
    will carry my signature.
I give you six sonorous syllables,
a gaze that always carries (like a wounded bird),
    tenderness.
An anxiety of warm and deep water.
A dark office where the only light is the one coming
    from my verses.

A very used thimble for your boring nights, a photograph of our children.
The most beautiful bullet of this pistol that is always
with me, the inerasable memory (always latent
and deep) of the children,
that one day, you and I conceived,
and the piece of life that I've got left,
this I give (convinced and happy) to the Revolution.
Nothing that can unite us can have greater strength.»

Undoubtedly, in the deepest part of Che Guevara's psyche, in
his final moments, a deep melancholy of defeat was beating
his soul down. To his wife he dedicates and offers tenderness
from his inner wounds, the darkness that surrounds him,
which seems more a simile for death, the memory of the
children conceived and the stunning confession of the last
bullet, as a premonition that he even lacked the strength to
use it.

In his last days to the north of the Grande River, high atop
the mountain ranges, the inhabitants, mostly indigenous
people, were fleeing in fear from Che's guerrilla troops. And
Che Guevara dies with the awareness of the rejection of the
peasants for his revolutionary project.

Indigenous people seem to fear long hair, thick beards and
the dirty and scruffy clothing worn by the guerrillas. In fact,
part of the guerrilla troops began to suffer from war stress, as
was the case of Olo Pantoja who would often see Bolivian
soldiers approaching but they were only in his imagination.
Even Pacho or Pachungo confesses in his diary that he feels

confused, because day and night turn one into the other. He accepts being surrounded by the army, and so he keeps his pistol ready to kill himself before being made prisoner.[1]

In this time of anguish, abandonment and human loneliness, Che Guevara's main concern was the death psychoses suffered by some of his lieutenants, in addition to the physical and mental weakness that was an impediment to making correct decisions. Che's emotions —in these last few days— seemed to be hurting and broken from all sides.

Once Manila —that is Fidel Castro and the the General Intelligence Directorate (DGI) of the Cuban Government— showed not the least bit of interest in reestablishing contact with Guevara and in doing all that was humanly and politically possible to extricate him from the predicament or thick Bolivian spiderweb in which he was in, the catastrophic end of Che Guevara and his Cuban and Bolivian guerrillas was at hand.

Benigno, one of the most loyal of Che's guerrilla fighters said on one occasion in an accusatory and frank way: «It seems as if Cuba wanted to get rid of us.»

But he went further, when in an act of brutal catharsis he added that this whole story, so filled with sufferings and deaths has one author, by the name of Fidel Castro.[2]

---

1. Fernández Montes de Oca. *El Diario de Pacho*. Editorial Punto y Coma, 1987 / pp. 9-99
2. Alarcón Ramírez, (Benigno) *Memorias de un Soldado*, Tusquets S.A, 1997 / p. 309

Let's look in a quick sequence with timely stops, at how this harsh statement by Benigno begins to turn with the passage events and years into a crushing truth:

«When Che arrived in the area of Ñancahuazú to visit farmer Honorato Rojas in the house selected to be his headquarters, called Calamine House, a brick house with zinc roof, he finds out directly from Rojas' comments, that the army was hardly 40 kilometers away building schools and roads.

And so Che Guevara comments with complete critical honesty to his followers: "and what the hell are we doing here if the army is so near and building a road."»

We already analyzed in the previous chapter how inconceivable, contradictory and even erratic it had been to set up Che Guevara's camp in Ñancahuazú, without previously assessing its objective disadvantages.

From his place of refuge in Moscow, years later, even Mario Monje would recognize that the decision to select Ñancahuazú and to purchase the farm with Calamine House in it, «was arbitrary, not strategic in the least.»

If this late recognition by Monje, which cost the lives of the Cuban guerrillas and hence Che Guevara's were to have any value of contrition, it would be a mortal blow to the ignominy of several people.

In the end what all this cruel reality showed in stark detail is that Mario Monje and the Bolivian Communist Party were aligned with the peaceful coexistence line of the Soviet

Union and were thus opposed to any guerrilla or subversive adventure in the continent.

We already know that in the preamble to Che Guevara's guerrilla project conceived from his exile in Prague —he had indicated his preference for Argentina or Perú for his guerrilla war, but the Government of Havana had opposed those destinations tenaciously and forcefully.

We are also aware of the suspicious contradiction of Fidel Castro telling Bolivian Mario Monje to help the revolutionary project in using Bolivian territory to reach Perú, but without mentioning the name of Guevara, while telling Che that the guerrilla project could not be in Perú, but rather in Bolivia and that it could count on the support of the Bolivian Communist Party.

Well, well, what an interesting hodgepodge of lies from all sides! This corroborates that Fidel Castro in fact lied to both without any kind of consideration in this preface so full of risks and supreme sacrifices.

Witness testimonies from close friends reveal that Che's refrain was to incessantly repeat that after Cuba his next destination was to «liberate» his native land, Argentina.[3]

However, the Congo definitively took him away from his homeland, because despite his insistence, he never got Fidel Castro to approve his prized objective.

Che Guevara's affliction at his flight from the Congo made

---

3. O'Donnelll, Pacho. *Che*, Editorial de Bolsillo, 2005 / pp. 396-398

him believe that the Cuban revolution was destined to stagnate due to its almost submissive dependency on the Soviet Union.[4]

Finally, the variant of a new guerrilla destination directs Che Guevara definitely to Bolivia, despite all its inherent contradictions.

Let's quickly go over how the whole trajectory of Che and his Cuban guerrillas in Bolivia became a veritable comedy of errors and mishaps for these men who aspired to organize the most important guerrilla movement in the history of the Americas, comparable only to Vietnam, according to Che's own prognostication.

However, the initiative ended up with a group of hungry and thirsty revolutionaries, without the least bit of hope of surviving militarily, in great measure because they didn't get the least bit of help from Bolivian peasants.

It becomes very meaningful that in the ten months of life of Che Guevara's guerrillas in Bolivia, not one Bolivian peasant voluntarily joined his irregular forces.

In Bolivia, Che made the same mistake he made in Congo, despite that in his memoir *Congo Diary*, he confides with total intellectual clarity that his big mistake was to erroneously trust in the fact that his mere presence in the Congo would attract the support of the Congolese, not discounting the errors that a certain amount of arrogance and feelings of

---

4. Ortega, Luis: *Yo soy el Che*, Ediciones Espuela de Plata, 2009 / p. 283

superiority in his command distanced him from reality, with the aggravating tendency to once again differentiate between Cuban fighters and the locals, which made more difficult the necessary integration of all fighters.[5]

To the tragic fault of a hypertrophied ego, and a relationship mishandled by headquarters, is added lack of terrain knowledge. But something that worsens this scenario is that Che arrived in Bolivian territory, as he did in the Congo, without the logistical support structure he enjoyed during the Cuban revolution of Fidel Castro, given the contributions that the 26th of July Movement directed by Frank País provided, as well as the peasants' structure coordinated by Crescencio Pérez, a sort of peasant patriarch, a leader in the Sierra Maestra known as «the bandit of the mountains» who had under him a group of between one and two thousand peasants throughout this mountainous area.[6]

Right from the start of their exploration of the terrain in February 1967 in the selected area of Ñancahuazú, Che's guerrilla is considered a strange group of fellows by their neighbors, who initially considered that they could possibly be drug traffickers, more likely than the pig farmers they were trying to pull off.

The same thing had happened to the Guevara-inspired guerrilla in Salta, Argentina, in September 1963, when a group

---

5. Guevara, Ernesto. *Pasajes de la Guerra Revolucionaria (Congo)*, Océano Sur, 2009 / pp. 242-257
6. Franqui, Carlos. *Retrato de familia con Fidel*, Editalorial Seix Barral, 1981 / p. 458

headed up by Jorge Massetti was defeated in the town of El Yuro.

In this first stage of Che in Bolivia, several guerrilla fighters drowned due to the excessive rigor that Guevara put them through on the scouting training marches. Additionally, two Bolivian guerrillas deserted, reporting to the army about the existence of an irregular cell. At the beginning of the month of March, some hunters and fishermen detected a group of three strange youngsters who acted like they were supposedly students of a university in Potosí, with a lot of money in cash and guns, triggering a call by the hunters to Army Fourth Division.

All this makes the Bolivian armed forces, less than three months after their arrival in the area, detect the existence of an irregular group as well as its location. When the army visited Calamine House, they found a pot with boiling water, a green-colored Jeep parked in the back and some personal objects.

The following day the Bolivian army returned to continue its investigation and then realized that the supposed occupants of the structure had left, taking with them all their household utensils.

With this preliminary investigation, the army confirmed the presence of irregulars in the area, and so Che decides to prepare an ambush, which takes place on March 23, where the scout of the group, an officer and five army soldiers, are killed and 14 are taken prisoner.

This guerrilla action was definitively erratic and hurriedly ordered by Che, triggering an official communiqué from the Bolivian government about the news, allowing the confirmation of the presence of guerrillas or bandits in the area.

For his part, the first guerrilla communiqué under the name of National Liberation Army, was not able to be transmitted, because the radio transmitter was broken and the original logistics had not foreseen sending alternative or substitute ones to the guerrilla.

This situation highlights that from the start in the Bolivian mountains, Che's Cuban guerrilla faced very grave communication and organizational issues as well as lack of logistics planning, which would get worse later.

In these early days, to provide more agility and penetration to his guerrilla group, Che divided his force into a forward section, made up of the Cubans Miguel Hernández Osorio, alias Manuel, Alberto Fernández Montes de Oca, alias Pachungo or Pacho and Daniel Alarcón Ramírez, alias Benigno, in addition to Bolivians Humberto Vazquez-Viaña, alias Loro, Aniceto Reinaga, alias Aniceto, David Adriazola, alias Dario, Raúl Quispaya Choque, alias Raúl and Orlando Bazán, alias Camba.

The central force was headed up by Che, with brothers René Martínez Tamayo, alias Arturo and José María Martínez Tamayo, alias Ricardo, Olo Pantoja, alias Antonio, Leonardo Tamayo, alias Urbano, Harry Villegas, alias Pombo and Octavio de la Concepción de la Pedraja, alias El Médico, El Moro or Morogoro, all Cubans. The Bolivians Roberto

Peredo, alias El Coco, Julio Méndez, alias El Ñato, Simeón Cuba Sarabia, alias Willy and Moisés Guevara, alias Moisés, made up the central nucleus.

In this force we have to include the presence of French writer Regis Debray, the Argentine painter Ciro Busto and the female guerrilla Tania, although these last three would later go to the rear group where Tania would eventually die.

And the rear, commanded by Juan Vitalio Acuña, alias Joaquín, was made up by Cubans Jesús Suárez Gayol, alias El Rubio, Gustavo Machín, Antonio Sánchez Díaz, alias Marcos, in addition to Bolivians Antonio Nuñez Tardío, alias Pan Divino, Apolinar Aquino Quispe, alias Apolinar and Casildo Condorí, alias Víctor, among others.

On April 10 Che's guerrilla made another tactical error in haste, a second ambush of the Bolivian army, where Jesús Suárez Gayol, alias El Rubio, a veteran revolutionary from the July 26th Movement was killed.

This ambush caused the government of General René Barrientos to ask for help from the U.S. government and the CIA, and so in a few weeks a group of U.S. Green Berets would arrive to train and put together the Second Ranger Battalion of the Bolivian Army.[7]

In this group of soldiers, headed by «Papi» Shelton, were Captains Edmond Fricke, Le Roy Mitchel and Margarito Cruz, 1st Lt. Harvey Wallender, Sergeants Oliveiro Gómez,

---

7. Weiss, Mitch & Maurer, Kevin. *Hunting Che*, Berkeley Publishers, 2013.

Rolando Milliard, Sergeants 1st Class, Daniel Chapa and Héctor Rivera, the former experts on light armaments and the latter in heavy armaments.

Also in the group were medical specialists, including, Jerald Petterson and James Hapta, in addition to radio operators Sergeants Wendell Thompson and Alvin Graham.

To this unit of Green Berets two CIA agents would then be added, Félix Rodríguez and Gustavo Villoldo, both Cubans and veterans of the Bay of Pigs invasion of 1961.

Later, on April 19, Che's guerrillas detained British journalist Andrew Roth, who was fulfilling a special mission to facilitate the tracking of the Cuban guerrillas for Bolivian and American intelligence services.

Now in this stage of the guerrilla war, Che resented the inconvenience of not having a radio transmitter to allow him to communicate with Cuba and the rest of the world, while the U.S. government was sending in a group of counterinsurgency veterans to help the Bolivian armed forces.

On the other hand, due to the schism with the Bolivian Communist Party, Guevara and his guerrilla were forced to recruit green Bolivians for the insurgency, through Maoist Communist union leader Moisés Guevara, which turned out to be a failure due to the weak commitment, inexperience and scant training that these men got for the hard work of the life of a guerrilla.

It is even known that from the middle of the month of March, the Criminal Investigation Directorate of the Bolivian

Interior Ministry was conducting a follow up investigation of this labor leader and had infiltrated two agents in the group of this Bolivian labor leader.

These two Bolivian moles, Vicente Rocabada Terrazas and Pastor Barrera Quintana, deserted in Camirí, reporting to the Fourth Army Division the presence of a group of Che Guevara guerrillas, the location of their camp, and the number of guerrillas in it.

Che's guerrilla war in Bolivia had started its first firefights in the month of March, and so Che Guevara's April summary in his field diary states the following: «Our isolation is still complete, illnesses have sapped the health of several comrades, forcing us to divide our forces, which have decreased a lot of our effectiveness; we have not been able to reach Joaquín; the peasant base is still to be developed; although through planned terror we will be able to neutralize most of it; their support would come later. Not one has joined up...»

Joaquín was a Cuban officer who had been designated by Che from the start to lead the rearguard group. Another grave inconvenience in this first sequence of important events was mentioned before –the departure from La Paz of liaison officer Renán Montero.

But even more serious than his departure was that no replacement for him had been planned, nobody was sent to become the new liaison. Che was left isolated in the Bolivian mountains to be on his own, without contact with La Paz or with Havana.

This decision to leave Che Guevara alone without a liaison in La Paz was worsened by the fact that the guerrilla group, as we said, had been left without a radio transmitter and no other equipment was on the way to replace it.

Hence, soon, Guevara was totally isolated in Bolivia, something that practically diminished his mobility, lacking the means to issue guerrilla actions and sources of communication for planning and ensuring supplies.

Facing this nebulous scenario, full of needs right from the start, Che committed a serious mistake in his guerrilla strategy in Bolivia, when he ordered French writer Regis Debray and Argentine painter Ciro Bustos, his main contacts for his guerrilla plans in Argentina to abandon the guerrilla in Ñancaguazú.

Guevara's reasoning in the face of his early isolation was for Debray to leave Bolivia and begin to construct an international campaign in favor of the guerrilla, at the same time taking a message to Fidel about the importance of reestablishing contacts, while Bustos would go back to reactivate the underground network in Argentina.

For the operation of facilitating the exit of Debray and Bustos from the Bolivian guerrilla, Che used a rearguard group led by Joaquín, which means that from the moment this tactical decision is made, the forward unit and the rearguard unit separate and lose contact. They would never reunite again.

Thus separated, despite Che's efforts and persistence, and those of Joaquín to join forces again, both brigades would find their annihilation.

Later it was learned, although not at the time, that the two groups were moving about very near each other, which evidences the gravity of the lack of terrain knowledge by the guerrilla had, as well as its lack of trustworthy scouts, updated maps, a base network of peasant support, effective radio transmitters, and regular contact with La Paz and Havana.

On April 20, Regis Debray and Ciro Bustos are dropped by the rearguard in the rural town of Muyupampa, and this unleashes the worst disaster in the life of the guerrilla, since both are quickly arrested by the Bolivian army and, during their interrogations, the presence of Cuban guerrillas in Bolivia is confirmed.

To make matters worse, painter Ciro Bustos drew a portrait of some of the guerrillas, and with his written deposition reconfirmed that Che was in Bolivian territory.

Also, according to the records from both depositions, it is known that Debray gave up a lot of inside information about his participation in the guerrilla, which makes Che state in his diary that «Debray talked too much.»

In this interview in 1968 for the U.S. magazine *Evergreen Review*, journalist George Andrew Roth confirmed that Regis

Debray told his interrogators about the presence of Che in Bolivia.[8]

With this information from Debray, alias Danton, the CIA, or part of the agency, finally buried its mistaken belief that Che could have died in the Congolese guerrilla war.

In the month of April, now already suffering food and asthma medicine shortages, Che's guerrilla suffers the casualty of Rolando, whose real-life name was Eliseo Reyes Rodríguez, another veteran of the Sierra Maestra.

«Dark day,» wrote Guevara in his field diary.

Hunger, lack of communication, thirst and a strong persecution from the Bolivian army continued to beat down both of the Cuban guerrilla's forward and rear columns.

«We are missing total peasant participation,» wrote Che in his diary on May 28. A few weeks later, on June 26, Carlos Coello, alias Tuma, one of Che's inseparable guerrillas dies in combat, and so he writes in his diary, «With him left me an inseparable comrade whose fidelity was proven beyond measure, whose absence I feel from now almost like that of a son.»

Some of the guerrillas present in Tuma's farewell record testimony of Che's tears at his death in combat.

During the month of July, Che ratified in his diary «The total lack of contact with the outside world» adding the impossi-

---

8. Interview with U.S. magazine. Evergreen Review, 1968.

of finding the rearguard guerrilla group, the lack of peasants joining the guerrilla and the loss of fighters.

On July 30 died guerrilla José María Martínez Tamayo, alias Papi, who was surprised in his camp by the Bolivian army.

According to Che himself, he was an undisciplined guerrilla, but an excellent fighter. With him also died the Bolivian guerrilla Raúl Quispaya Choque, a man belonging to Moisés Guevara's Maoist group.

«We are now 22, with three crippled, including me, which slows down our mobility» wrote Guevara in his diary.

In the month of August, Che is nearing his end, recognizing the «lowering of fighting morale» and again ratifies that «we are still without any sort of contact.»

It's worthwhile to note that according to an old legal adage «Confession of the parties relieves the presentation of evidence» and that due to the isolation they were enduring, the fighting morale of Che's guerrilla in Bolivia was at its lowest level.

We reached the end of August and according to many eyewitnesses, the demoralization of Che Guevara's guerrillas was thorough. They kept on losing valuable men, betrayals were continuous, hunger extremely debilitated them, they lacked water and Che was going on without asthma medicine, as the persistent isolation kept on physically and morally wearing down and grinding down the guerrillas.

From the statement in his diary: «We continue lacking any sort of contact and without the reasonable expectation to establish it soon. There is fighting fatigue.»

It was a very demoralizing stage for the guerrillas who had to sacrifice horses and mules to eat meat, according to their own statements.

During those days, Che lost his emotional control stabbing his own mare which he was riding for going too slowly. After this emotional outburst, came the news that the other rearguard guerrilla group under the command of Joaquín had been annihilated in the area of the town of Muyupampa.

All this was due to the betrayal of Honorato Rojas, the peasant that took them to the banks of the Grande River, an area controlled by the Army's 8th Division.

In this ambush, which was really a massacre and a bad omen for Che Guevara's guerrillas. Fighters Tania Bunker, Gustavo Machín and Moisés Guevara, among others, died.

Initially, Che could not believe the news of the total annihilation of the guerrilla brigade that covered his rearguard. With this defeat, the Cuban guerrilla had lost a third of its forces. Their deformed and decaying corpses were displayed in the laundry room of Nuestro Señor de Malta Hospital, for the townspeople to be aware of the presence of guerrillas in the area.[9]

Among the objects that Lt. Col. Selich kept after the ambush

---

9. O'Donnelll, *Pacho*: Ibid, 2005 / p. 483

where Che's rearguard completely perished, was a poem from Tania the Guerrilla, which goes like this:

«Don't' leave guitar man,

As the light of my soul goes out,

I want to return at dawn

To die among the Cacharpayas».

Cacharpaya is an Andean festival that features singing and dancing to bid farewell to a loved one. Although Che was upset at Tania for having abandoned her intelligence work in La Paz to physically join the guerrilla without his permission, there is no doubt that he must have deeply felt the death of this German woman, who had trusted him and his project unconditionally.

Some very close to Che Guevara and his ramblings around the world assure that in the first stages of his revolutionary relationship the two had been lovers.

In September the media began to run reports that the army had Che and his guerrillas encircled. At that time, the incorporation of two Cuban CIA agents was confirmed, in order to collaborate with the Bolivian army in the capture of Che Guevara.

They were Félix Rodríguez and Gustavo Villoldo, both veteran anti-Communist fighters against the Fidel Castro regime, who had arrived in La Paz in early August taking a very active part in finding and capturing Che.

At the same time, now in the month of September, the presence in the Bolivian army of U.S. Green Berets was revealed, led by the veteran Papi Shelton and Capt. Leroy Mitchell, previously mentioned, as counterinsurgency instructors in the Bolivian army, to fight Che's Cuban guerrillas.

Later documents, such as statements by Leonid Brezhnev, Prime Minister of the USSR, that the guerrilla activities in Bolivia «were prejudicial to the true interests of the Communist cause» are a reflection that explains the effort that the Soviet KGB must have undertaken, in parallel with the CIA, to achieve the defeat of Che's Cuban guerrilla.[10]

Both intelligence agencies considered Che Guevara a person of courage, smarts, and explosive dangerousness. Due to the constant harassment of the Bolivian army, Che decided to leave the Grande River, heading for the mountain ranges farther north, mainly inhabited by indigenous people.

The guerrilla's climb to the north was chaotic, as they lacked enough energy, food, water, and what was crucial for Che, asthma medicine.

One extraordinary incident came to aggravate Che's emotional mood as well as that of his trusted staff, since in mid September in La Paz, a young Bolivian woman whom Che had designated as the treasurer of the guerrilla, Loyola Guzmán, was captured.

Guzmán tried to commit suicide jumping off a third-floor

---

10. Castañeda, Jorge G. *La vida en rojo*, Alfaguara, 1997 / p. 468

window at the Ministry of the Interior to avoid being tortured and forced to blow the whistle on her guerrilla comrades, but she survived.

In their flight to the north of the Grande River, Che and his diminished forces arrived in the hamlet of Alto Seco, 2,000 meters above sea level.

Che confessed that during the march, he observed how frightened people would move away from the guerrillas. At this point in time, the army already had information that the Cuban guerrilla was moving extremely slowly, among other reasons, because Che's sickness made him have to ride a horse.

Later statements by guerrilla survivors vouch for the fact that Che already lacked the strength to walk, was wounded in the shoulder, was in a deplorable mood, in addition to having lost his boots, having to tie rags made of sacks to try to fashion a pair of espadrilles that could cover up the sores on his feet.

Before arriving in the hamlet of Alto Seco, the army already knew that the guerrillas were in the area. Che himself, due to his exhaustion, hunger, thirst, asthma and low morale, was violating one of the most elemental principles of guerrilla warfare, ordering to walk in plain sight, without care for the presence of strangers or of the Bolivian army.

Upon arrival in the town of La Higuera, the guerrilla forces fell into an ambush in which the Cuban Manuel Hernández

Osorio, alias Manuel and Bolivians Roberto Peredo, alias Coco and Mario Gutiérrez, alias Julio, were killed.

After this disastrous situation, Bolivians Camba (Orlando Jiménez Bazán) and León (Antonio Domínguez Flores), took advantage of a slip to desert.

Che and some of his men, with great effort and exhausted, were able to flee to a mountain canyon, farther to the north, where they hid for two or three days.

Looking forward to Che Guevara's capture and the annihilation of the Cuban guerrilla in Bolivia, Bolivian President René Barrientos arrived in Vallegrande with his staff and aides.

On October 7 the guerrillas, under the leadership of a despairing Che Guevara slowly worked their way through a gap near La Higuera.

The following day at Churo Ravine, an intense firefight broke out between the army, led by Capt. Gary Prado and the Cuban guerrilla force, where two guerrillas René Martínez Tamayo, alias Arturo and Antonio Sánchez Díaz, alias Pinares were killed.

Che was left wounded in the calf, losing his M-2 carbine, damaged by a bullet that had hit the barrel of his rifle. However, his pistol, and its cartridge were in good condition.

A few minutes later Sergeant Bernardino Huance, of indigenous ancestry, appeared from behind some bushes pointing his rifle at Che.

We cannot help but record the mysterious phrase that Che told his captor at the precise moment of his capture, since it contradicts his systematic preaching to his followers to never allow themselves to be captured by the enemy. Che said: «Don't shoot, don't shoot, I am Che Guevara, and I am worth more alive than dead.»

The mystery is left to speculation because the bullet that Che carried in his pistol didn't activate. And he would be the only one to explain his most intimate motivation in not taking his life.

Almost all his biographers coincide in that Che Guevara is captured as a veritable human skeleton, in the greatest state of misery, lacking boots, food, being dirty and smelly, without any type of contact with La Paz or with his supposed comrades in Havana, or what is worse, anguished by an asthma that had reduced him to guttural sounds as he gasped for a bit of air.

In this latest combat Cuban guerrillas Arturo (Martínez Tamayo) and Orlando (Olo Pantoja) had died. Che, now in custody, is bound by hands and feet inside the school at La Higuera.

That evening, Lt. Col. Andrés Selich asked where President René Barrientos was and what he was to do with Che Guevara.

Following this, in the company of other officers, Selich approached Che asking him why he was so depressed. To which Che replied, «Because I have failed.»

There the Bolivian officers began to read Che's notes in his field diary until the early morning hours. In the early morning of October 9 a helicopter landed at La Higuera carrying Col. Joaquín Zenteno and Capt. Ramos, who in fact was the Cuban CIA agent Félix Rodríguez.

According to a later report by Félix Rodríguez, Che looked like a beggar, dirty and haggard, and additionally he was wounded and bloodied, with dirty rags tied around his feet.

Rodríguez recounts how he immediately got busy photographing the pages of Che's Diary, once he had reported to the CIA base the capture of the Argentine guy.

At noon on that October 9, Col. Zenteno Anaya gave the order to commander Ayoroa to take charge of proceeding with the summary execution of Che.

According to later testimonies by Lt. Col. Selich, both he, as well as CIA officer Félix Rodríguez, were of the view of not executing Che, as they thought it was more profitable to have him alive than dead.

The Central Intelligence Agency, CIA, offered Col. Zenteno Anaya an airplane to transfer Che to Panamá, but he replied to the them that he could not disobey an order from the President, General René Barrientos.

At 13:10 of October 9, 1967, Che Guevara was executed with several shots to the chest delivered by a sergeant of small stature, Mario Terán, who had volunteered to do it.

On October 10, with the corpse of Che Guevara in Valle-grande, General Ovando Candía ordered the amputation of his two hands as proof of death.

All seems to indicate that these Bolivian military men who ordered to cut off Che's hands thought that this act of human mutilation would silence the memory of the Argentine guer-rilla fighter.

They were wrong, it didn't turn out that way, as Che's memory flew like the Phoenix bird to remain in safekeeping in the minds of millions of youth around the world who have continued to venerate him for having surrendered his life for his ideas.

Had he been tried by competent Bolivian courts, as should have happened, Che would have appeared as an incompe-tent and bloody interloper in a majority indigenous and poor country, in addition to his frightened final moments where he displayed more a wish to live than to die.

It is precisely here, at this ruinous junction of loss of human lives on both sides, that the myth of Che Guevara is born, with many young people around the world uplifting his memory with veneration and respect.

With his death, Che showed that he could be an excellent theoretician for his guerrilla focal point fronts, but that in fact he was a very bad operator and leader to successfully carry out any type of similar enterprise.

His guerrilla strategy failed spectacularly in Salta, Argentina, in Congo, Africa and at La Higuera, Bolivia. Of course we need to talk about his supposed allies in this project —Fidel Castro and the Communist Party of Bolivia— who rather than allies turned into accomplices of his most determined enemy, the Soviet intelligence KGB.

It stands as a sad paradox that the Central Intelligence Agency, the US CIA, would be the only institution in the world to intercede before the Bolivian military to save the life of Che Guevara.[11]

The CIA agreed with Che Guevara that he was worth more alive than dead...

---

11. Rodríguez, Félix and Weisman, John. *Shadow Warrior*, New York, Simon & Schuster, 1989.

6

THE ABANDONMENT

CHE CAST A VERY LARGE SHADOW OVER FIDEL. REASONS FOR THE ABANDONMENT. POEM TO JESUS CHRIST

«Fidel needed to get rid of Che.»

(Benigno, a Che lieutenant in Bolivia and a guerrilla in the Sierra Maestra, Cuba)

This research is ending, after a long journey scrutinizing the facts, reading through essays, very different biographies and after reviewing the extensive correspondence regarding Che, in search of a logical and coherent approximation regarding why he died in the Bolivian mountains, isolated from the world and as if a beggar, with hardly a piece of bread to take to his mouth.

As previous events and without any apparent connection to the guerrilla disaster in Bolivia, but intimately related with the common denominator of failure, we have Che's diary while in his guerrilla journeys in Africa, entitled Congo Diary which we have already noted.

This memoir of the Congo curiously took the government in Havana forty years to publish. Nobody knows for sure why the delay, but there remains the doubtful speculation of biographers and researchers.

Some of the more perspicacious historians point to an intentional objective—in not publishing it— of hiding the deep disgust of Che Guevara, stated in his memoirs, regarding the decision of the government in Havana, without first consulting him, to order the end of guerrilla operations in Congo. Also not published in Cuba has been the complete exchange of letters between Che Guevara and his mother Celia. It is known of one letter from Che to his mother, before leaving for the African continent, where he tells her of some friction with the government of Fidel Castro asking her not to travel to Cuba until he gets back to her.

Word got out about this letter from Che to his mother announcing a strange trip abroad by a letter of reply that Celia sent her son in Havana. It is symptomatic too that these letters have not been published in Cuba.[1]

Celia expressed in an extract from her letter to her son. «Who has been judged to be correct, or given primacy, regarding the dispute of the reasons that ought to be reasons for granting incentives?» which shows that she knew the crux of the large discrepancy regarding volunteer work and about

---

1. Constenla, Julia. Celia, *La madre del Che*, Editorial Suramericana, 2004 / p. 263

the Sino-Soviet schism that separated her son from Fidel
Castro at that time.[2]

We pause or jump to the recent past to reinforce some perti-
nent events in the historical panorama for his research work.
We add two premonitory anecdotes. The first took place on
January 6, 1959 in the city of Cienfuegos, when Fidel Castro
met with the commanders of the Escambray Second Front,
Lázaro Ascencio and Armando Fleites, because it paints a
picture in advance of an event of historical significance,
similar to the one we are trying to fathom in this book
regarding the death of Che Guevara.[3]

The two commanders, old and close friends of Fidel Castro
since college days, asked for the meeting. During it, Ascencio
told Fidel that the greatest worry facing the revolutionaries
belonging to the Escambray Second Front was the Communist danger that lurked over Cuba and its revolution.

To this Fidel replied without missing a beat «don't worry, the
only Communists in the revolution are my brother Raúl and
Che Guevara, and as far as Raúl one slap in the face will
shake off his pretensions of power, while I will send Che to a
far-away guerrilla front for the Imperialist to do him in.»

This verbatim anecdote could well remain inside a fragile
and even humorous anthology of anecdotes if we didn't know
of more elements to understand the genesis of these links in
the development of the stormy guerrilla process that led Che

2. O'Donnelll, Pacho. *Che*, Editorial Debolsillo, 2005 / pp. 34 -348
3. Report of direct conversation with Armando Fleitas, rebel commander

Guevara to meet his death in Bolivia, without the expected solidarity of his closest revolutionary comrades from Havana.

Of course, the real trigger in this historical comment by Fidel Castro to Ascencio and Fleites perfectly fits with later developments since scarcely two years later the Cuban revolution took on a tilt, turning Communist, by the expressed decision of the very same Fidel Castro, with the backing of his most radical lieutenants.

What is interesting about Fidel's comments to Ascencio and Fleites is the similarity with what in fact took place later with Che Guevara at La Higuera, with his dramatic circumstance of dying without the awaited support of the revolutionary government in Havana.

The second anecdote took place months later, but it presents an astonishing similarity with the first. The leaders of the July 26th Movement, Vicente Báez, Emilio Guedes and Horacio Fernández Vila met with Fidel Castro to bring up the preoccupation of many leaders of the revolutionary organization regarding how Communists, with the support of Raúl Castro and Che Guevara, were infiltrating the Cuban Revolution at all levels.

To this Fidel replied that that attitude on the part of Raúl and Che was bordering on treason, asking them for trust and time to solve the problem.[4]

The sequence of events or links that made possible the aban-

---

4. Guedes, Emilio. *Cuba, la revolución que no fue*, Eriginal Books, 2013/ p.702

of Che Guevara, which caused his tragic death on Bolivian soil, are known and are readily available to be evaluated with the greatest possible objectivity. Let's review these links in as great a detail as possible:

The first link to the abandonment

This first link is the most important one as it causes a pivotal point in the distancing and discrepancy between Fidel Castro and Ernesto (Che) Guevara, and it centers around the speech by Che Guevara at the Afro-Asian Conference in Algeria (February 24, 1965) when, with a peculiar license and sincerity, he raised his voice to strongly criticize the Soviets as being Imperialists and Mercantilists, simply comparing them to the United States.[5]

This speech produced the first accusation, from Raúl Castro, with Fidel's acquiescence during the tense meeting the three held at his return from Algiers, that Che was a pro-Chinese Trotskyite who was placing relations between the Cuban revolution and the USSR in danger, at a time when Fidel Castro was beginning to weave a close relationship with the top leadership of the Soviet Union.

At the shouts of Raúl Castro accusing Che of being a Trotskyite, Che responded angrily: «you are stupid, you are stupid». Then Che left the meeting slamming the door on their faces.

This accusation by Raúl Castro that Che was a sympathizer

---

5. Speech by Che Guevara at the Algiers Conference. (See Document Section)

of the People's Republic of China and not of the Soviet Union would follow Ernesto Guevara for the rest of his revolutionary life.

From that moment on, Che Guevara began to disappear from the public scene in Cuba. This creates a climate of rumors, social unrest and certain spontaneous expectations. The first version launched, handled by the revolutionary government and its intelligence networks, is that Guevara had gone out to cut sugarcane in the eastern provinces. Both the U.S. Central Intelligence Agency and the KGB then raised their antennas to find out the real location of the Argentine commander.

Even the American leftist magazine 'Monthly Review' publicly asked: «Is Fidel Castro really aware of what is really at stake in the case of Guevara? Does he realize that every delay in clearing up the mystery adds to the anguish and doubts of honest revolutionaries, to the satisfaction of his enemies?»

The Soviet ambassador to Cuba, Alexander Alexeiev, aware of the importance of Che's departure from the public scene, asked Fidel Castro directly about Che's whereabouts, during a sugarcane cutting workday in Camagüey.

Fidel took him aside and told him in a whisper, «Che is not cutting cane in Oriente, he is off to Africa. I don't want you to speak about this by radio or in code, but I want you to tell your leaders in person when you can.»

So directly, without subterfuge or cover up, Fidel Castro, in person, tells the Ambassador of the Soviet Union in Cuba,

Alexander Alexeiev, the man charged with informing the Soviet Intelligence Agency, KGB, that Che is in the Congo and not cutting sugarcane during the Cuban sugar harvest.[6]

At the same time, during this stage, Fidel was beginning to weave a complex web of friendships and economic agreements with the Soviet Union within the complex scenario of the Cold War, despite the fact that many old Communist cadres within the most rancid orthodoxy of the Socialist Popular Party of Cuba (the old Cuban Communist Party) were planning to overthrow him considering him an improvised dictator lacking in Marxist training.

From this time on, Che begins to turn into a controversial element for the Cuban government apparatus led by Fidel Castro, who looked to an alliance with the Soviet Union as a savior, despite the fact that this relationship of dependency with the Soviets had its well-known moments of tension between Fidel and the very Soviet leadership.

Fidel then publicly assumes in a speech delivered on July 26, 1965 in Santa Clara, an ideological position opposite that of Che Guevara attacking moral incentives and centralized administration in a show of quick rapprochement with the basic economic tenants of the USSR.

The distancing between Fidel and Che is clearly evident in the makeup of the first Central Committee recently created by the PCC, the Communist Party of Cuba in 1965, on October 1, when none of Che's right-hand men who were

---

6. Castañeda, Jorge G. *La vida en rojo*, Alfaguara, 1997/ p. 370

government ministers were selected to belong to the leadership of this new party organism.

Excluded were Luis Álvarez Rom, Finance Minister; Orlando Borrego, Sugar Minister, and Arturo Guzmán, Industry Minister, the three leaders close to Che Guevara.

Another one to be excluded from the Central Committee was Arturo Villaseca, a personal friend and mathematics teacher of Che, who was a former director of the National Bank.

But Che didn't back down from this distancing with Fidel Castro, as in an interview that he granted at the time to the Uruguayan magazine *Marcha*, he charged again with his criticisms of material incentives implemented by the Yugoslavs, which in these terms agreed with the Soviet Union.

After these incidents, Che Guevara disappeared from the Cuban public stage to never return again.

The second link to the abandonment

A second link to Che's abandonment focuses on the erroneous and suspicious selection of Bolivia as the appropriate place to organize a guerrilla where to send Che, as this country provided the least conditions for a guerrilla project of this nature.

What is to explain that the Cuban Central Intelligence (CID) and Fidel Castro did not discard prima facie a country such as Bolivia, which they knew and had so stated, did not present the conditions required for a guerrilla uprising?

At the same time, a secret report issued in 1966 by the Central Intelligence Agency (CIA) explained that Bolivia was the Latin American country in least danger and presenting the least conditions for the development of an irregular guerrilla movement.[7]

The reasons, shared by all political analysts of the time and of the region were that Bolivia, ever since its nationalist revolution in 1952 led by Víctor Paz Estensoro, had distributed land to the peasants by means of an Agrarian Reform, hence the country lacked conditions for a quick incorporation of the peasants into any revolutionary call.

All these facts obviously presented objective difficulties for the selection of Bolivia as the indicated place for a guerrilla movement designed from Havana.

To this is added the rare slip up by the Cuban Central Intelligence Department in the preparation of the guerrilla theater of operation in Ñancahuazú, in sending two huge, heavy, WWII-vintage old tube radio transmitters needing a strong generator to operate.

One of these old radio transmitters was stored in a cave, where it was drenched with water and stopped working. Then two tubes broke from the second radio transmitter and it was unable to ever broadcast again, leaving Che without communication, starting in the month of February in the mountains of Bolivia.

---

7.   Rostow, Walter. *Walter Rostow to the President, Secret*, October 18, 1967

All this, from the very month of February was fully realized by Fidel Castro as well as by any and all Cuban officials who had anything to do with Che Guevara's guerrilla project in Bolivia.

At the end of his life, Guevara only had with him a small 6-band radio receiver which could not send any messages and was only used to listen to Radio Havana. Why didn't Fidel Castro and the Cuban Central Intelligence Department not plan to send modern radio transmitters, well-equipped and in sufficient numbers to substitute for any flaw or loss in combat, before the arrival of Che in Bolivia?

This being another question that has not had a logical or coherent answer.

The third link to the abandonment

At this stage in the sequence of links to the abandonment, we are obliged to pause as it is the most suspicious human element, among all mentioned, which was the selection of Mario Monje and the Bolivian Communist Party as Che's allies to develop the revolutionary project in Bolivia.

At that time, almost all Communist parties in Latin America, including the one in Bolivia, were signing into an alliance in favor of peaceful coexistence inspired by the Soviet Union, despite the enormous sympathies that the Cuban revolution evoked on Latin American youth since 1959.

This alignment of the Communist parties throughout the Continent with the Soviet-sponsored peaceful coexistence thesis is what makes the Cuban government of Fidel Castro's efforts contradictory in stimulating and forcing this alliance to support and consolidate Che Guevara's guerrilla project in Bolivia.

That is why this link is so damming, because it uncovers the frailty of an alliance that never really existed or that only lived inside the cold and calculating mind of a Fidel Castro who preferred —in agreement with the leaders of the Soviet Union— to have Che Guevara far away from the inner circle of the Cuban Revolution in Havana.

Mario Monje, more concerned with boycotting the guerrilla project than in helping it along, was the person that decided to buy the farm in Ñancahuazú, convincing Guevara's lieutenants that it was the most adequate place.

Later on, Monje himself, as we wrote before, had the audacity to confess in an interview published in Moscow, that the selection and purchase of the farm in Ñancahuazúan with Calamine House in it, didn't follow any serious analysis of responsibility or logistics.

Upon arrival in Bolivia, as was seen in the previous chapter, Che Guevara himself realized that the place was not adequate, that the area lacked peasants, and that very near the Bolivian Army was constructing military camps.

To all this is added that French writer Regis Debray, sent to Bolivia on the orders of Fidel Castro and the Central Intelligence Department (CID) with the objective to evaluate the best location for Che Guevara's guerrilla camp, was categorical in his report in recommending the areas of Alto Beni or

Los Yungas, as the most propitious and advantageous on account of their climate and rural conditions, both very distant from the one selected by Mario Monje.

Additionally, the areas recommended by Debray were located near Perú, which was Che's second objective, once Argentina had been discarded due to Fidel Castro's iron-hand refusal. All this demonstrates the dubious nature of selecting, as principal allies of Che Guevara's guerrillas in Bolivia, a Bolivian Communist Party absolutely in fealty to the strategic line of «peaceful coexistence» advocated by the Soviet Union.

The fourth link to the abandonment

The most irritating of all in this search around the links that try to explain the reasons for abandoning Che Guevara in Bolivia, is the strong evidence that neither Fidel Castro not the General Inteligence Directorate (DGI) in Havana showed any interest in solidarity to a rescue of the Argentine guerrilla when everyone knew that his stay in Bolivia was precarious, highly dangerous and almost suicidal.

In fact Fidel Castro and the Central Intelligence Department did the opposite to that which they should have done to try to rescue Che Guevara, because they moved some of the pieces off the board, like ordering Renán Montero, alias Iván, Cuba's link to La Paz and a high-ranking officer in Cuban intelligence, to leave Bolivia, when this contact was needed the most to protect the guerrilla project.

This evidence, by itself, without mentioning the others, places Cuban official entities, headed by Fidel Castro, as the principal axis in Che Guevara's abandonment in the mountains of Bolivia.

Regarding Montero's abrupt exit from La Paz, two reasons that carry little weight have been advanced by the Government of Fidel Castro. The first is that Montero was travelling to Paris to legalize some documents and some expired passports.

The second is that he was ill, but none of these two reasons sound convincing, as a few months later Montero was sent to Nicaragua to actively collaborate with the Farabundo Martí Front of El Salvador.

It is also known from Benigno and other high-ranking Cuban officers, that a group of Cuban officers had been organized in Havana to go rescue Che Guevara in Bolivia.

This group of rescuers were led by commanders Juan Carretero, alias Ariel, later to become Cuba's ambassador in Iraq, in addition to high-ranking Cuban officers, Armando Campos and Enrique Acevedo.[8]

They had come up with an alternative rescue plan to extricate Che Guevara from the Bolivian mountains, which was known by Commander Manuel Piñeiro, head of the Central Intelligence Department, but it was disarticulated by the express orders of Fidel Castro, no explanation needed.

---

8. Alarcón, Ramírez, (Benigno). *Memoria de soldado cubano*, Tusquets, 1997/pp. 186

However, the following year Fidel Castro authorized the rescue of 24 Cuban guerrillas encircled in the mountains of Venezuela, where Commander Arnaldo Ochoa was serving.

Obviously, Fidel Castro took an interest in saving Commander Ochoa, but that was not his attitude when it came to rescuing Che Guevara in the Bolivian mountains, whose rescue plan was disparaged.

Che's charges in Algiers were not only pointing to the Soviets as mean, but also accused them of being accomplices to the Imperialist exploitation, similar to the one carried out by the U.S.

According to an interview granted by Algerian President Ahmed Ben Bella in 1964, «Che had complete awareness of the surprise he would cause in various circles and in the straits he would place Fidel Castro and the Cuban revolution. The Soviets already had Che Guevara in their sights for his Trotskyite waywardness, his real sympathy for the Chinese, his trips to Beijing, his African wanderings and his tenacious opposition to Russian recommendations for the Cuban economy, which had occasioned strong doses of ill will in Moscow.»

In a later attempt to try to moderate Che's position towards the Soviet Union, Fidel decided to send him to Moscow in November 1964 to celebrate the 47th Anniversary of the Bolshevik Revolution and the opening of the Cuban-Soviet Friendship House.

Che didn't pass over the opportunity in Moscow to mediate in the Sino-Soviet conflict, something that the Soviet leadership found very distasteful.

During this trip, Che found out first hand that the Soviets counted on the loyal and unconditional support of almost all Latin American Communist parties in the strategy of peaceful coexistence rejecting any guerrilla insurgency in Latin America.

This explains how during a speech in Santiago de Cuba on November 30, 1964, now back in Cuba, Che criticized the refusal of Latin American Communist parties to collaborate in armed struggle following the peaceful coexistence strategy of the USSR.

At this time the distancing of the two most salient figures of the Cuban Revolution began to be well defined between Che Guevara and Fidel Castro.

Meanwhile, another emotional incident that produced a reasonable amount of indignation was when the health of Celia, the mother of Ernesto Guevara in Argentina turned for the worse, and the family tried to call Havana to talk to Che, but from Havana the reply was curt and disproportionately cold, including Aleida March's, the wife of Che, as all told Guevara's relatives that «they were unable to locate Che.»

Celia died desperately trying to find out about her son, but not even his great revolutionary friend, Ricardo Rojo was able to break the wall of silence that Cuba put up on that occasion.

A letter from Celia, published by Rojo three years later in his book *Mi amigo el Che*, sadly showed that her mother's intuition told her that her son had trouble with Fidel Castro.[9]

At this stage we have to ask ourselves a more disquieting question in this investigation, whether Che's abandonment in Bolivia was conscious or a simple accumulation of coincidences and mistakes.

With his critical posture against the Soviets and the United States, as if they were two similar imperialisms, Guevara gains a dimension of immeasurable popularity among the young and the left throughout the world. Not so Fidel, which one considerable sector of the left begins to see as a Communist autocrat for his support of the Soviet invasion of Czechoslovakia, and for his repressive and systematic persecution of homosexuals in Cuba and his contempt for the followers of John Lennon in the Island.

This contrast of differences between Che and Fidel is not something that is easy for Fidel Castro to digest, whose personality was showing a strong bent for egocentrism and authoritarianism.

That is why if we isolate the main factors that prove the abandonment, as a hypothesis for political analysis, we see

---

9. Lee Anderson, John. *Che Guevara*, Grove Press, New York, 1997 / pp. 606–607

how each of these factors searches for and links to the other strongly and with spontaneity.

Let us review the way in which Fidel Castro, in his long life as revolutionary leader from the halls of the University of Havana to the death of Che at La Higuera, going through the uplifting experience of turning into a respected revolutionary leader among the revolutionaries of the world, had the ability and skill to physically or morally erase all his adversaries or dissidents that would dare to doubt his revolutionary credibility and power, or to simply compete with him.

Let's look at only a few examples, since the list of those eliminated by Fidel Castro is too long and with the cases we will mention it will become clear to the reader that the Cuban commander-in-chief has never allowed any dissidence or discrepancies even if the name of Che Guevara is attached to them.

First on the list of those sacrificed, as reported by *Hoy*, the official newspaper of the former Partido Socialista Popular de Cuba (the Communist Party at the time) dated February 26, 1948 provides plenty of precise details regarding the presentation of charges against Fidel Castro and others accused in the murder of the college leader Manolo Castro in the University of Havana.

Manolo Castro was an unimpeachable student leader who became the first victim of Fidel Castro and a group of friends. In the end, due to his absolutist political ambitions, Fidel Castro cannot stand having a charismatic and much beloved figure such as Manolo Castro in the campus of the University of Havana.

At the end of the judicial process it was found that although Fidel Castro was not the one that shot Manolo Castro to kill him, it was indeed one of his group of college friends.

Fidel Castro's group is also accused of the assassination of a university police sergeant by the name of Oscar Fernández Caral, a few weeks before Manolo Castro's assassination.

At that time Fidel Castro joined irregular groups of revolutionaries in Havana, some having the profile of gangsters, something well-defined in Cuban history.

In 1959, very soon after the revolutionary triumph, Fidel Castro ordered the jailing and prison sentence of 20 years for one of his most well-respected lieutenants in the Sierra Maestra, Commander Húber Matos.

The reason for the prison sentence for Matos was that he had sent a resignation letter to Fidel denouncing the dangers that Communists posed to the Cuban Revolution.

On October 12, 1960, Fidel Castro ordered the execution of the Revolutionary Commander Porfirio Remberto Ramírez, President of the College Student Federation in the University of Las Villas, for opposing the Communist tilt of the 1959 Cuban revolution.

In that same year 1960, Fidel Castro ordered the sentencing to political prison for the simple act of trying to leave the country of labor leader David Salvador, First Secretary

General of the Cuban Workers Confederation. He was the top union leader in the July 26th Movement.

On April 17, 1961, Fidel Castro ordered University of Havana student leaders Virgilio Campanería Ángel and Alberto Tapia Ruano to face the firing squad for trying to oppose his attempts to divert the Cuban revolution towards Communism.

On April 20, 1961, Fidel Castro ordered the death by firing squad of Humberto Sorí Marín, Minister of Agriculture and principal strategist of the 1959 Agrarian Reform Act, for revolutionary activities against allowing the Cuban revolution to take a surprising turn towards Communism.

Together with Sorí Marín, other well-known Cuban revolutionaries were shot, including Eufemio Fernández, Rogelio Fernández Corso, alias Francisco, Manuel Puig and Rafael Díaz Hanscom, all opposed to the turn towards Marxist Communist that the Cuban revolution was taking.

On March 11, 1961, Fidel Castro ordered the death by firing squad of Alexander (William) Morgan, a military man who had participated in the Cuban Revolution. Fidel used to call him «Comandante Yankee» having earned the title of «Hero of the Cuban Revolution» in 1959.

In the month of May 1961, Fidel Castro ordered the death by firing squad in Santiago de Cuba of Rebel Army Capt. Fernando del Valle Galindo, a right-hand man of David Salvador, the jailed 26th of July Movement labor leader.

On March 13, 1963, Fidel Castro ordered the death by firing squad of revolutionary Ricardo Olmedo, who in 1957 had participated in the assault against the Presidential Palace to execute dictator Fulgencio Batista.

On May 25, 1972, Pedro Luis Boitell, a college student leader and member of the 26th of July Movement died. Fidel had ordered several weeks before to let him die of hunger as he was holding a prolonged hunger strike of more than seven weeks in protest for the mistreatment of political prisoners.

On November 13, 1989, Fidel Castro ordered the death by firing squad of General Arnaldo Ochoa, the most prestigious officer in the Cuban Revolutionary Armed Forces, for his supposed link to drug trafficking and emerald traffic.

However, Ochoa's closest colleagues profess that Fidel Castro's order was really connected with the general's sympathies for the reforms imposed by Mikhail Gorbachev in the Soviet Union.

Together with General Ochoa Col. Antonio de la Guardia, and Capts. Jorge Martínez and Amado Padrón faced the firing squad, all revolutionaries in the inner circle of Gen. Arnaldo Ochoa.

In the early morning hours of July 13, 1994, Fidel Castro ordered four vessels equipped with water hoses to sink the Remolcador (Tugboat) 13 de Marzo which was trying to escape Cuba with 72 people aboard, leaving a total of 41 people dead, including 10 children.

Some analysts of the Cuban situation believe that this was one of the most denigrating and genocidal acts of Fidel Castro during his more than half a century in power.

On April 11, 2003, Fidel Castro ordered the death by firing squad of three black Cubans, Bárbaro Leodán, Lorenzo Copello Castillo and Jorge Luis Martínez Issac, for the simple act of trying to leave the country.

We stop this unfinished list here as it is not the goal of this book to relate the execution of thousands, as well as the story of those jailed or eliminated who shared this sad ending, which compares the personality of Fidel Castro well with the trajectory of dictator Joseph Stalin of the Soviet Union.

Of course, the death of Che Guevara did not occur facing a firing squad nor did it take place after a long prison sentence, but it could have ended in this very well crafted operation by Fidel Castro with the okay of the Soviet Union to eliminate once and for all this pesky Argentine guerrilla leader.

Can these links be tied to the complicity of Fidel Castro? At least that is the opinion of Benigno, one of Che's main lieutenants, when he expressed with singular realism his opinion that «Fidel needed to get rid of Che.»

According to Benigno, Fidel Castro didn't want him alive, as this represented very real challenges, which were uncomfortable for him. He preferred to have him dead, because, among other things, Che was casting a shadow on him, being a transparent revolutionary that didn't condescend to Soviet power, regardless of how powerful it might be.

That is why he left him on his own, and the death of Guevara may seem to be a meticulous plan with no escape route. That is how Benigno sees it, because all the links took him to that gloomy conclusion that Fidel Castro wanted him dead or disappeared to ingratiate himself with the Soviets, who hated Guevara for his militant Trotskyism.

To this is added that the Soviets did all that was humanly possible to effect the destruction of Che Guevara in Bolivia, which they were finally able to achieve with the help of Mario Monje and the Communist Party of Bolivia.

Of course, due to his intelligence and astuteness, Fidel still had a card left, which he played masterfully, using Che's memory for his own propaganda purposes. He has used it, despite all the links to the abandonment that we have demonstrated.

If we look over Che's Bolivia Diary, the most compromising constant regarding his abandonment is repeated by Che with alarming and accusatory frequency almost every month: «we are still waiting for contact with Manila (Fidel).»

Che's Bolivia diary is the greatest prosecutor against Fidel Castro; no subterfuge or speculation or inventions are required. The document is available to all. Read it.

Che Guevara died at a crucial moment in contemporary history. The young people of the world, students and workers showed solidarity and activism during the Prague Spring. Protests seeking a better world took place in all the important cities on the planet.

The music of the Beatles became the liberation rhythm of the time in all corners of the world. The sexual revolution reached its greatest aspirations for a greater freedom of gender. The decade of the 1960s left behind a cultural aspiration that is contagious, of which there are still living and lasting traits.

Che's death inserted itself properly in the aspirations of the young people of the earth, while Fidel Castro in Cuba was cruelly persecuting homosexuals, jailing the followers of John Lennon, and providing solidarity for the Soviet invasion of Czechoslovakia, as he consolidated his repressive regime in the Island of Cuba, only to be topped by Joseph Stalin in the land of the Soviets.

Che Guevara continues to be an icon in the world, despite his unnecessary and hateful harshness in La Cabaña Fortress in Havana and in other places, because culturally he inserted himself in that wave of rebellious expression of the 1960s. A true myth that must end when freedom returns to Cuba.[10]

That is why some like Benigno and others believe that Fidel Castro ordered the abandonment of Che in Bolivia as well as maliciously preparing the previous incursion in the Congo in 1964 which almost cost the life of the Argentine guerrilla.

Fidel Castro needed to get rid of Che, because he couldn't stand being overshadowed by his prestige and intellectual honesty, or on account of his international leadership among

---

10. Ros, Enrique, *Ernesto Guevara, Mito y Realidad*, Ediciones Universal, 2003/ pag.13

the young, as was courageously denounced by Benigno, one of his most trusted aides.

In the same way that Fidel Castro jailed Húber Matos, one of the most prestigious commanders in the Sierra Maestra; and as he turned Rafael del Pino into a martyr, one of his best friends from youth until he provoked his suicide; and as he had Arnaldo Ochoa shot, the most respected general in Cuba on account of his courage and professionalism, allegedly for a supposed contraband in diamonds and drugs; and as so many others, in 1967 at La Higuera, dejected and abandoned it was Che Guevara's turn.

Each reader can draw his or her own conclusion, but the elements of this historical research are sufficiently convincing and strong to clear away any doubt.

It's interesting to note that the last thoughts that Che Guevara had in the mountains of Bolivia were not about Fidel Castro or the Cuban Revolution, but rather to the merciful image of Jesus of Nazareth. That is why he bids farewell with a poem to Christ.

We close this book with the suggestive poem by León Felipe, dedicated to the figure of Jesus of Nazareth that Che rewrote in his last days or hours of life, as is related by one of his most eminent biographers, the Argentine writer Pacho O'Donnell.

This poem, according to Pacho O'Donnell, was found in the guerrillas backpack, once dead:

Christ, I love you,
Not because you came down from a star,
But because you revealed to me
That man has tears, grief.
Yes, you taught me that man is God, a poor
crucified God like you.

What an anguish revealing document selected by Che to say good-bye!

DOCUMENTS AND NOTES

a. List of documents

1. Speech by Che at the Afro-Asian Conference in Algeria (1965)
2. Speech by Che at the UN (1964)
3. Farewell letter from Che to Fidel
4. Poem by Che to his wife Aleida March
5. Poem by Che to Jesus of Nazareth (rewritten from a poem by poet León Felipe).
6. Tale by Che dedicated to his mother Celia, La Piedra
7. Note by Che in the Congo about the death of his mother Celia
8. Memorandum from CIA Director

Seech by Che Guevara at the Afro-Asian Conference in Algeria (February 24, 1965)

Source: *The Che Reader*, Ocean Press, © 2005.
Transcription/Markup: Ocean Press/Brian Baggins
Copyright: © 2005 Aleida March, Che Guevara Studies Center and Ocean Press.

Cuba is here at this conference to speak on behalf of the peoples of Latin America. As we have emphasized on other occasions, Cuba also speaks as an underdeveloped country as well as one that is building socialism.

It is not by accident that our delegation is permitted to give its opinion here, in the circle of the peoples of Asia and Africa. A common aspiration unites us in our march toward the future: the defeat of imperialism. A common past of struggle against the same enemy has united us along the road.

This is an assembly of peoples in struggle, and the struggle is developing on two equally important fronts that require all our efforts. The struggle against imperialism, for liberation from colonial or neocolonial shackles, which is being carried out by means of political weapons, arms, or a combination of the two, is not separate from the struggle against backwardness and poverty. Both are stages on the same road leading toward the creation of a new society of justice and plenty.

It is imperative to take political power and to get rid of the oppressor classes. But then the second stage of the struggle, which may be even more difficult than the first, must be faced.

Ever since monopoly capital took over the world, it has kept the greater part of humanity in poverty, dividing all the profits among the group of the most powerful countries. The standard of living in those countries is based on the extreme poverty of our countries. To raise the living standards of the underdeveloped nations, therefore, we must fight against imperialism. And each time a country is torn away from the imperialist tree, it is not only a partial battle won against the main enemy but it also contributes to the real weakening of that enemy, and is one more step toward the final victory. There are no borders in this struggle to the death. We cannot be indifferent to what happens anywhere in the world, because a victory by any country over imperialism is our victory, just as any country's defeat is a defeat for all of us. The practice of proletarian internationalism is not only a duty for the peoples struggling for a better future, it is also an inescapable necessity.

If the imperialist enemy, the United States or any other, carries out its attack against the underdeveloped peoples and the socialist countries, elementary logic determines the need for an alliance between the underdeveloped peoples and the socialist countries. If there were no other uniting factor, the common enemy should be enough.

Of course, these alliances cannot be made spontaneously, without discussions, without birth pangs, which sometimes can be painful. We said that each time a country is liberated it is a defeat for the world imperialist system. But we must agree that the break is not achieved by the mere act of proclaiming independence or winning an armed victory in a revolution. It is achieved when imperialist economic domination over a people is brought to an end. Therefore, it is a matter of vital interest to the socialist countries for a real break to take place. And it is our international duty, a duty determined by our guiding ideology, to contribute our efforts to make this liberation as rapid and deep-going as possible.

A conclusion must be drawn from all this: the socialist countries must help pay for the development of countries now starting out on the road to liberation. We state it this way with no intention whatsoever of blackmail or dramatics, nor are we looking for an easy way to get closer to the Afro-Asian peoples; it is our profound conviction. Socialism cannot exist without a change in consciousness resulting in a new fraternal attitude toward humanity, both at an individual level, within the societies where socialism is being built or has been built, and on a world scale, with regard to all peoples suffering from imperialist oppression.

We believe the responsibility of aiding dependent countries must be approached in such a spirit. There should be no more talk about developing mutually beneficial trade based on prices forced on the backward countries by the law of value and the international relations of unequal exchange that result from the law of value.

How can it be «mutually beneficial» to sell at world market prices the raw materials that cost the underdeveloped countries immeasurable sweat and suffering, and to buy at world market prices the machinery produced in today's big automated factories?

If we establish that kind of relation between the two groups of nations, we must agree that the socialist countries are, in a certain way, accomplices of imperialist exploitation. It can be argued that the amount of exchange with the underdeveloped countries is an insignificant part of the foreign trade of the socialist countries. That is very true, but it does not eliminate the immoral character of that exchange.

The socialist countries have the moral duty to put an end to their tacit complicity with the exploiting countries of the West. The fact that the trade today is small means nothing. In 1959 Cuba only occasionally sold sugar to some socialist bloc countries, usually through English brokers or brokers of other nationalities. Today 80 percent of Cuba's trade is with that area. All its vital supplies come from the socialist camp, and in fact it has joined that camp. We cannot say that this entrance into the socialist camp was brought about merely by the increase in trade. Nor was the increase in trade brought about by the destruction of the old structures and the adoption of the socialist form of development. Both sides of the question intersect and are interrelated.

We did not start out on the road that ends in communism foreseeing all steps as logically predetermined by an ideology advancing toward a fixed goal. The truths of socialism, plus the raw truths of imperialism, forged our people and showed them the path that we have now taken consciously. To advance toward their own complete liberation, the peoples of Asia and Africa must take the same path. They will follow it sooner or later, regardless of what modifying adjective their socialism may take today.

For us there is no valid definition of socialism other than the abolition of the exploitation of one human being by another. As long as this has not been achieved, if we think we are in the stage of building socialism but instead of ending exploitation the work of suppressing it comes to a halt — or worse, is reversed — then we cannot even speak of building socialism.[23] We have to prepare conditions so that our brothers and sisters can directly and consciously take the path of the complete abolition of exploitation, but we cannot ask them to take that path if we ourselves are accomplices in that exploitation. If we were asked what methods are used to establish fair prices, we could not answer because we do not know the full scope of the practical problems involved. All we know is that, after political discussions, the Soviet Union and Cuba have signed agreements advantageous to us, by means of which we will sell five million tons of sugar at prices set above those of the so-called free world sugar market. The People's Republic of China also pays those prices when buying from us.

This is only the beginning. The real task consists of setting prices that will permit development. A great shift in ideas will be involved in changing the order of international relations. Foreign trade should not determine policy, but should, on the contrary, be subordinated to a fraternal policy toward the peoples.

Let us briefly analyze the problem of long-term credits for developing basic industries. Frequently we find that beneficiary countries attempt to establish an industrial base disproportionate to their present capacity. The products will not be consumed domestically and the country's reserves will be risked in the undertaking.

Our thinking is as follows: The investments of the socialist states in their own territory come directly out of the state budget, and are recovered only by use of the products throughout the entire manufacturing process, down to the finished goods. We propose that some thought be given to the possibility of making these kinds of investments in the underdeveloped countries. In this way we could unleash an immense force, hidden in our continents, which have been exploited miserably but never aided in their development. We could begin a new stage of a real international division of labor, based not on the history of what has been done up to now but rather on the future history of what can be done.

The states in whose territories the new investments are to be made would have all the inherent rights of sovereign property over them with no payment or credit involved. But they would be obligated to supply agreed-upon quantities of products to the investor countries for a certain number of years at set prices.

The method for financing the local portion of expenses incurred by a country receiving investments of this kind also deserves study. The supply of marketable goods on long-term credits to the governments of underdeveloped countries could be one form of aid not requiring the contribution of freely convertible hard currency.

Another difficult problem that must be solved is the mastering of technology. The shortage of technicians in underdeveloped countries is well known to us all. Educational institutions and teachers are lacking. Sometimes we lack a real understanding of our needs and have not made the decision to carry out a top-priority policy of technical, cultural and ideological development.

The socialist countries should supply the aid to organize institutions for technical education. They should insist on the great importance of this and should supply technical cadres to fill the present need. It is necessary to further emphasize this last point. The technicians who come to our countries must be exemplary. They are comrades who will face a strange environment, often one hostile to technology, with a different language and totally different customs. The technicians who take on this difficult task must be, first of all, communists in the most profound and noble sense of the word. With this single quality, plus a modicum of flexibility and organization, wonders can be achieved.

We know this can be done. Fraternal countries have sent us a certain number of technicians who have done more for the development of our country than 10 institutes, and have contributed more to our friendship than 10 ambassadors or 100 diplomatic receptions.

If we could achieve the above-listed points — and if all the technology of the advanced countries could be placed within reach of the underdeveloped countries, unhampered by the present system of patents, which prevents the spread of inventions of different countries — we would progress a great deal in our common task.

Imperialism has been defeated in many partial battles. But it remains a considerable force in the world. We cannot expect its final defeat save through effort and sacrifice on the part of us all.

The proposed set of measures, however, cannot be implemented unilaterally. The socialist countries should help pay for the development of the underdeveloped countries, we agree. But the underdeveloped countries must also steel their forces to embark resolutely on the road of building a new society — whatever name one gives it — where the machine, an instrument of labor, is no longer an instrument for the exploitation of one human being by another. Nor can the confidence of the socialist countries be expected by those who play at balancing between capitalism and socialism, trying to use each force as a counterweight in order to derive certain advantages from such competition. A new policy of absolute seriousness should govern the relations between the two groups of societies. It is worth emphasizing once again that the means of production should preferably be in the hands of the state, so that the marks of exploitation may gradually disappear. Furthermore, development cannot be left to complete improvisation. It is necessary to plan the construction of the new society. Planning is one of the laws of socialism, and without it, socialism would not exist. Without correct planning there can be no adequate guarantee that all the various sectors of a country's economy will combine harmoniously to take the leaps forward that our epoch demands.

Planning cannot be left as an isolated problem of each of our small countries, distorted in their development, possessors of some raw materials or producers of some manufactured or semi-manufactured goods, but lacking in most others. From the outset, planning should take on a certain regional dimension in order to inter-mix the various national economies, and thus bring about integration on a basis that is truly of mutual benefit. We believe the road ahead is full of dangers, not dangers conjured up or foreseen in the distant future by some superior mind but palpable dangers deriving from the realities besetting us. The fight against colonialism has reached its final stages, but in the present era colonial status is only a consequence of imperialist domination. As long as imperialism exists it will, by definition, exert its domination over other countries. Today that domination is called neocolonialism.

Neocolonialism developed first in South America, throughout a whole continent, and today it begins to be felt with increasing intensity in Africa and Asia. Its forms of penetration and development have different characteristics. One is the brutal form we have seen in the Congo. Brute force, without any respect or concealment whatsoever, is its extreme weapon. There is another more subtle form: penetration into countries that win political independence, linking up with the nascent local bourgeoisies, development of a parasitic bourgeois class closely allied to the interests of the former colonizers. This development is based on a certain temporary rise in the people's standard of living, because in a very backward country the simple step from feudal to capitalist relations marks a big advance, regardless of the dire consequences for the workers in the long run.

Neocolonialism has bared its claws in the Congo. That is not a sign of strength but of weakness. It had to resort to force, its extreme weapon, as an economic argument, which has generated very intense opposing reactions. But at the same time a much more subtle form of neocolonialism is being practiced in other countries of Africa and Asia. It is rapidly bringing about what some have called the South Americanization of these continents; that is, the development of a parasitic bourgeoisie that adds nothing to the national wealth of their countries but rather deposits its huge ill-gotten profits in capitalist banks abroad, and makes deals with foreign countries to reap more profits with absolute disregard for the welfare of the people. There are also other dangers, such as competition between fraternal countries, which are politically friendly and sometimes neighbors, as both try to develop the same investments simultaneously to produce for markets that often cannot absorb the increased volume. This competition has the disadvantage of wasting energies that could be used to achieve much greater economic coordination; furthermore, it gives the imperialist monopolies room to maneuver.

When it has been impossible to carry out a given investment project with the aid of the socialist camp, there have been occasions when the project has been accomplished by signing agreements with the capitalists. Such capitalist investments have the disadvantage not only of the terms of the loans

but other, much more important disadvantages as well, such as the establishment of joint ventures with a dangerous neighbor. Since these investments in general parallel those made in other states, they tend to cause
divisions between friendly countries by creating economic rivalries.
Furthermore, they create the dangers of corruption flowing from the
constant presence of capitalism, which is very skillful in conjuring up
visions of advancement and well-being to fog the minds of many people.
Some time later, prices drop in the market saturated by similar products.
The affected countries are obliged to seek new loans, or to permit additional
investments in order to compete. The final consequences of such a policy
are the fall of the economy into the hands of the monopolies, and a slow but
sure return to the past. As we see it, the only safe method for investments is
direct participation by the state as the sole purchaser of the goods, limiting
imperialist activity to contracts for supplies and not letting them set one foot
inside our house. And here it is just and proper to take advantage of inter-
imperialist contradictions in order to secure the least burdensome terms.

We have to watch out for «disinterested» economic, cultural and other aid
that imperialism grants directly or through puppet states, which gets a
better reception in some parts of the world.

If all of these dangers are not seen in time, some countries that began their
task of national liberation with faith and enthusiasm may find themselves on the neocolonial road, as monopoly domination is subtly established step by step so that its effects are difficult to discern until they
brutally make themselves felt.

There is a big job to be done. Immense problems confront our two worlds —
that of the socialist countries and that called the Third World — problems directly concerning human beings and their welfare, and related to
the struggle against the main force that bears the responsibility for our
backwardness. In the face of these problems, all countries and peoples
conscious of their duties, of the dangers involved in the situation, of the
sacrifices required by development, must take concrete steps to cement
our friendship in the two fields that can never be separated: the
economic and the political. We should organize a great solid bloc that, in
its turn, helps new countries to free themselves not only from the political power of imperialism but also from its economic power.

The question of liberation by armed struggle from an oppressor political
power should be dealt with in accordance with the rules of proletarian

internationalism. In a socialist country at war, it would be absurd to conceive of a factory manager demanding guaranteed payment before shipping to the front the tanks produced by his factory. It ought to seem no less absurd to inquire of a people fighting for liberation, or needing arms to defend its freedom, whether or not they can guarantee payment. Arms cannot be commodities in our world. They must be delivered to the peoples asking for them to use against the common enemy, with no charge and in the quantities needed and available. That is the spirit in which the Soviet Union and the People's Republic of China have offered us their military aid. We are socialists; we constitute a guarantee of the proper utilization of those arms. But we are not the only ones, and all of us should receive the same treatment.

The reply to the ominous attacks by U.S. imperialism against Vietnam or the Congo should be to supply those sister countries with all the defense equipment they need, and to offer them our full solidarity without any conditions whatsoever.

In the economic field we must conquer the road to development with the most advanced technology possible. We cannot set out to follow the long ascending steps from feudalism to the nuclear and automated era. That would be a road of immense and largely useless sacrifice. We have to start from technology at its current level. We have to make the great technological leap forward that will reduce the current gap between the more developed countries and ourselves. Technology must be applied to the large factories and also to a properly developed agriculture. Above all, its foundation must be technological and ideological education, with a sufficient mass base and strength to sustain the research institutes and organizations that have to be created in each country, as well as the men and women who will use the existing technology and be capable of adapting themselves to the newly mastered technology.

These cadres must have a clear awareness of their duty to the society in which they live. There cannot be adequate technological education if it is not complemented by ideological education; without technological education, in most of our countries, there cannot be an adequate foundation for industrial development, which is what determines the development of a modern society, or the most basic consumer goods and adequate schooling. A good part of the national revenues must be spent on so-called unproductive investment in education. And priority must be given to the development of agricultural productivity. The latter has reached truly incredible levels in many capitalist countries, producing the senseless crisis of overproduction and a surplus of grain and other food products or industrial raw materials in the developed countries. While the rest of the world goes hungry, these countries have enough land and labor to produce several times over what is needed to feed the entire world. Agriculture must be considered a fundamental pillar of our development. Therefore, a fundamental aspect of our work should be changes in the agrarian structure, and adaptation to the new technological possibilities and to the new obligations of eliminating the exploitation of human beings.

Before making costly decisions that could cause irreparable damage, a careful survey of the national territory is needed. This is one of the preliminary steps in economic research and a basic prerequisite for correct planning. We warmly support Algeria's proposal for institutionalizing our relations. We would just like to make some supplementary suggestions: First: in order for the union to be an instrument in the struggle against imperialism, the cooperation of Latin American countries and an alliance with the socialist countries is necessary.

Second: we should be vigilant in preserving the revolutionary character of the union, preventing the admission into it of governments or movements not identified with the general aspirations of the people, and creating mechanisms that would permit the separation from it of any government or popular movement diverging from the just road.

Third: we must advocate the establishment of new relations on an equal footing between our countries and the capitalist ones, creating a revolutionary jurisprudence to defend ourselves in case of conflict, and to give new meaning to the relations between ourselves and the rest of the world. We speak a revolutionary language and we fight honestly for the victory of that cause. But frequently we entangle ourselves in the nets of an international law created as the result of confrontations between the imperialist powers, and not by the free peoples, the just peoples, in the course of their struggles.

For example, our peoples suffer the painful pressure of foreign bases established on their territories, or they have to carry the heavy burden of massive foreign debts. The story of these throwbacks is well known to all of us. Puppet governments, governments weakened by long struggles for liberation or the operation of the laws of the capitalist market, have allowed treaties that threaten our internal stability and jeopardize our future. Now is the time to throw off the yoke, to force renegotiation of oppressive foreign debts, and to force the imperialists to abandon their bases of aggression. I would not want to conclude these remarks, this recitation of concepts you all know, without calling the attention of this gathering to the fact that Cuba is not the only Latin American country; it is simply the only one that has the opportunity of speaking before you today. Other peoples are shedding their blood to win the rights we have. When we send our greetings from here, and from all the conferences and the places where they may be held, to the heroic peoples of Vietnam, Laos, so-called Portuguese Guinea, South Africa, or Palestine — to all exploited countries fighting for their emancipation — we must simultaneously extend our voice of friendship, our hand and our encouragement, to our fraternal peoples in Venezuela, Guatemala and Colombia, who today, arms in hand, are resolutely saying «No!» to the imperialist enemy.

Few settings from which to make this declaration are as symbolic as Algiers, one of the most heroic capitals of freedom. May the magnificent Algerian people — schooled as few others in sufferings for independence, under the decisive leadership of its party, headed by our dear **compañero** Ahmed Ben Bella — serve as an inspiration to us in this fight without quarter against world Imperialism.

I. Speech by Che Guevara at the UN (December 11, 1964)

Source: **The Che Reader**, Ocean Press, © 2005.
Transcription/Markup: Ocean Press/Brian Baggins
Copyright: © 2005 Aleida March, Che Guevara Studies Center and Ocean Press. Reprinted with their permission..

Mr. President;

Distinguished delegates:

The delegation of Cuba to this Assembly, first of all, is pleased to fulfill the agreeable duty of welcoming the addition of three new nations to the important number of those that discuss the problems of the world here. We therefore greet, in the persons of their presidents and prime ministers, the peoples of Zambia, Malawi and Malta, and express the hope that from the outset these countries will be added to the group of Nonaligned countries that struggle against imperialism, colonialism and neocolonialism.

We also wish to convey our congratulations to the president of this Assembly [Alex Quaison-Sackey of Ghana], whose elevation to so high a post is of special significance since it reflects this new historic stage of resounding triumphs for the peoples of Africa, who up until recently were subject to the colonial system of imperialism. Today, in their immense majority these peoples have become sovereign states through the legitimate exercise of their self-determination. The final hour of colonialism has struck, and millions of inhabitants of Africa, Asia and Latin America rise to meet a new life and demand their unrestricted right to self-determination and to the independent development of their nations.

We wish you, Mr. President, the greatest success in the tasks entrusted to you by the member states.

Cuba comes here to state its position on the most important points of controversy and will do so with the full sense of responsibility that the use of this rostrum implies, while at the same time fulfilling the unavoidable duty of speaking clearly and frankly.

We would like to see this Assembly shake itself out of complacency and move forward. We would like to see the committees begin their work and not stop at the first confrontation. Imperialism wants to turn this meeting into a pointless oratorical tournament, instead of solving the serious problems of the world. We must prevent it from doing so. This session of the Assembly should not be remembered in the future solely by the number 19 that identifies it. Our efforts are directed to that end.

We feel that we have the right and the obligation to do so, because our country is one of the most constant points of friction. It is one of the places where the principles upholding the right of small countries to sovereignty are put to the test day by day, minute by minute. At the same time our country is one of the trenches of freedom in the world, situated a few steps away from U.S. imperialism, showing by its actions, its daily example, that in the present conditions of humanity the peoples can liberate themselves and can keep themselves free.

Of course, there now exists a socialist camp that becomes stronger day by day and has more powerful weapons of struggle. But additional conditions are required for survival: the maintenance of internal unity, faith in one's own destiny, and the irrevocable decision to fight to the death for the defense of one's country and revolution. These conditions, distinguished delegates, exist in Cuba.

Of all the burning problems to be dealt with by this Assembly, one of special significance for us, and one whose solution we feel must be found first — so as to leave no doubt in the minds of anyone — is that of peaceful coexistence among states with different economic and social systems. Much progress has been made in the world in this field. But imperialism, particularly U.S. imperialism, has attempted to make the world believe that peaceful coexistence is the exclusive right of the earth's great powers. We say here what our president said in Cairo, and what later was expressed in the declaration of the Second Conference of Heads of State or Government of Nonaligned Countries: that peaceful coexistence cannot be limited to the powerful countries if we want to ensure world peace. Peaceful coexistence must be exercised among all states, regardless of size, regardless of the previous historical relations that linked them, and regardless of the problems that may arise among some of them at a given moment.

At present, the type of peaceful coexistence to which we aspire is often violated. Merely because the Kingdom of Cambodia maintained a neutral attitude and did not bow to the machinations of U.S. imperialism, it has been subjected to all kinds of treacherous and brutal attacks from the Yankee bases in South Vietnam.

Laos, a divided country, has also been the object of imperialist aggression of every kind. Its people have been massacred from the air. The conventions concluded at Geneva have been violated, and part of its territory is in constant danger of cowardly attacks by imperialist forces.

The Democratic Republic of Vietnam knows all these histories of aggression as do few nations on earth. It has once again seen its frontier violated, has seen enemy bombers and fighter planes attack its installations and U.S. warships, violating territorial waters, attack its naval posts. At this time, the threat hangs over the Democratic Republic of Vietnam that the U.S. war makers may openly extend into its territory the war that for many years they have been waging against the people of South Vietnam. The Soviet Union and the People's Republic of China have given serious warnings to the United States. We are faced with a case in which world

peace is in danger and, moreover, the lives of millions of human beings
in this part of Asia are constantly threatened and subjected to the whim
of the U.S. invader.

Peaceful coexistence has also been brutally put to the test in Cyprus, due to
pressures from the Turkish Government and NATO, compelling the
people and the government of Cyprus to make a heroic and firm stand in
defense of their sovereignty.

In all these parts of the world, imperialism attempts to impose its version of
what coexistence should be. It is the oppressed peoples in alliance with
the socialist camp that must show them what true coexistence is, and it
is the obligation of the United Nations to support them.

We must also state that it is not only in relations among sovereign states that
the concept of peaceful coexistence needs to be precisely defined. As
Marxists we have maintained that peaceful coexistence among nations
does not encompass coexistence between the exploiters and the
exploited, between the oppressors and the oppressed. Furthermore, the
right to full independence from all forms of colonial oppression is a
fundamental principle of this organization. That is why we express our
solidarity with the colonial peoples of so-called Portuguese Guinea,
Angola and Mozambique, who have been massacred for the crime of
demanding their freedom. And we are prepared to help them to the
extent of our ability in accordance with the Cairo declaration.

We express our solidarity with the people of Puerto Rico and their great
leader, Pedro Albizu Campos, who, in another act of hypocrisy, has been
set free at the age of 72, almost unable to speak, paralyzed, after spending
a lifetime in jail. Albizu Campos is a symbol of the as yet unfree but
indomitable Latin America. Years and years of prison, almost unbear-
able pressures in jail, mental torture, solitude, total isolation from his
people and his family, the insolence of the conqueror and its lackeys in
the land of his birth — nothing broke his will. The delegation of Cuba,
on behalf of its people, pays a tribute of admiration and gratitude to a
patriot who confers honor upon our America.

The United States for many years has tried to convert Puerto Rico into a
model of hybrid culture: the Castilian language (aka «Spanish») with
English inflections, the Castilian language with hinges on its backbone
— the better to bow down before the Yankee soldier. Puerto Rican
soldiers have been used as cannon fodder in imperialist wars, as in

Korea, and have even been made to fire at their own brothers, as in the massacre perpetrated by the U.S. Army a few months ago against the unarmed people of Panama — one of the most recent crimes carried out by Yankee imperialism. And yet, despite this assault on their will and their historical destiny, the people of Puerto Rico have preserved their culture, their Latin character, their national feelings, which in themselves give proof of the implacable desire for independence lying within the masses on that Latin American island. We must also warn that the principle of peaceful coexistence does not encompass the right to mock the will of the peoples, as is happening in the case of so-called British Guiana. There the government of Prime Minister Cheddi Jagan has been the victim of every kind of pressure and maneuver, and independence has been delayed to gain time to find ways to flout the people's will and guarantee the docility of a new government, placed in power by covert means, in order to grant a castrated freedom to this country of the Americas. Whatever roads Guiana may be compelled to follow to obtain independence, the moral and militant support of Cuba goes to its people.

Furthermore, we must point out that the islands of Guadalupe and Martinique have been fighting for a long time for self-government without obtaining it. This state of affairs must not continue. Once again we speak out to put the world on guard against what is happening in South Africa. The brutal policy of apartheid is applied before the eyes of the nations of the world. The peoples of Africa are compelled to endure the fact that on the African continent the superiority of one race over another remains official policy, and that in the name of this racial superiority murder is committed with impunity. Can the United Nations do nothing to stop this?

I would like to refer specifically to the painful case of the Congo, unique in the history of the modern world, which shows how, with absolute impunity, with the most insolent cynicism, the rights of peoples can be flouted. The direct reason for all this is the enormous wealth of the Congo, which the imperialist countries want to keep under their control. In the speech he made during his first visit to the United Nations, **compañero** Fidel Castro observed that the whole problem of coexistence among peoples boils down to the wrongful appropriation of other peoples' wealth. He made the following statement: «End the philosophy of plunder and the philosophy of war will be ended as well.»

But the philosophy of plunder has not only not been ended, it is stronger than ever. And that is why those who used the name of the United Nations to commit the murder of Lumumba are today, in the name of the defense of the white race, murdering thousands of Congolese. How can we forget the betrayal of the hope that Patrice Lumumba placed in the United Nations? How can we forget the machinations and maneuvers that followed in the wake of the occupation of that country by UN troops, under whose auspices the assassins of this great African patriot acted with impunity? How can we forget, distinguished delegates, that the one who flouted the authority of the UN in the Congo — and not exactly for patriotic reasons, but rather by virtue of conflicts between imperialists — was Moise Tshombe, who initiated the secession of Katanga with Belgian support? And how can one justify, how can one explain, that at the end of all the United Nations' activities there, Tshombe, dislodged from Katanga, should return as lord and master of the Congo? Who can deny the sad role that the imperialists compelled the United Nations to play?

To sum up: dramatic mobilizations were carried out to avoid the secession of Katanga, but today Tshombe is in power, the wealth of the Congo is in imperialist hands — and the expenses have to be paid by the honorable nations. The merchants of war certainly do good business! That is why the government of Cuba supports the just stance of the Soviet Union in refusing to pay the expenses for this crime.

And as if this were not enough, we now have flung in our faces these latest acts that have filled the world with indignation. Who are the perpetrators? Belgian paratroopers, carried by U.S. planes, who took off from British bases. We remember as if it were yesterday that we saw a small country in Europe, a civilized and industrious country, the Kingdom of Belgium, invaded by Hitler's hordes. We were embittered by the knowledge that this small nation was massacred by German imperialism, and we felt affection for its people. But this other side of the imperialist coin was the one that many of us did not see. Perhaps the sons of Belgian patriots who died defending their country's liberty are now murdering in cold blood thousands of Congolese in the name of the white race, just as they suffered under the German heel because their blood was not sufficiently Aryan. Our free eyes open now on new horizons and can see what yesterday, in our condition as colonial slaves, we could not observe:

that «Western Civilization» disguises behind its showy facade a picture
of hyenas and jackals. That is the only name that can be applied to those
who have gone to fulfill such «humanitarian» tasks in the Congo. A
carnivorous animal that feeds on unarmed peoples. That is what imperialism does to men. That is what distinguishes the imperial «white man.»
All free men of the world must be prepared to avenge the crime of the
Congo. Perhaps many of those soldiers, who were turned into sub-
humans by imperialist machinery, believe in good faith that they are
defending the rights of a superior race. In this Assembly, however, those
peoples whose skins are darkened by a different sun, colored by different
pigments, constitute the majority. And they fully and clearly understand
that the difference between men does not lie in the color of their skin,
but in the forms of ownership of the means of production, in the relations of production. The Cuban delegation extends greetings to the
peoples of Southern Rhodesia and South-West Africa, oppressed by
white colonialist minorities; to the peoples of Basutoland, Bechuana-
land, Swaziland, French Somaliland, the Arabs of Palestine, Aden and
the Protectorates, Oman; and to all peoples in conflict with imperialism
and colonialism. We reaffirm our support to them.
I express also the hope that there will be a just solution to the conflict facing
our sister republic of Indonesia in its relations with Malaysia. Mr. President: One of the fundamental themes of this conference is general and
complete disarmament. We express our support for general and
complete disarmament. Furthermore, we advocate the complete destruction of all thermonuclear devices and we support the holding of a
conference of all the nations of the world to make this aspiration of all
people a reality. In his statement before this assembly, our prime
minister warned that arms races have always led to war. There are new
nuclear powers in the world, and the possibilities of a confrontation are
growing. We believe that such a conference is necessary to obtain the
total destruction of thermonuclear weapons and, as a first step, the total
prohibition of tests. At the same time, we have to clearly establish the
duty of all countries to respect the present borders of other states and to
refrain from engaging in any aggression, even with conventional
weapons.
In adding our voice to that of all the peoples of the world who ask for
general and complete disarmament, the destruction of all nuclear arse-

nals, the complete halt to the building of new thermonuclear devices and of nuclear tests of any kind, we believe it necessary to also stress that the territorial integrity of nations must be respected and the armed hand of imperialism held back, for it is no less dangerous when it uses only conventional weapons. Those who murdered thousands of defenseless citizens of the Congo did not use the atomic bomb. They used conventional weapons. Conventional weapons have also been used by imperialism, causing so many deaths.

Even if the measures advocated here were to become effective and make it unnecessary to mention it, we must point out that we cannot adhere to any regional pact for denuclearization so long as the United States maintains aggressive bases on our own territory, in Puerto Rico, Panama and in other Latin American states where it feels it has the right to place both conventional and nuclear weapons without any restrictions. We feel that we must be able to provide for our own defense in the light of the recent resolution of the Organization of American States against Cuba, on the basis of which an attack may be carried out invoking the Rio Treaty. If the conference to which we have just referred were to achieve all these objectives — which, unfortunately, would be difficult — we believe it would be the most important one in the history of humanity. To ensure this it would be necessary for the People's Republic of China to be represented, and that is why a conference of this type must be held. But it would be much simpler for the peoples of the world to recognize the undeniable truth of the existence of the People's Republic of China, whose government is the sole representative of its people, and to give it the seat it deserves, which is, at present, usurped by the gang that controls the province of Taiwan, with U.S. support.

The problem of the representation of China in the United Nations cannot in any way be considered as a case of a new admission to the organization, but rather as the restoration of the legitimate rights of the People's Republic of China.

We must repudiate energetically the «two Chinas» plot. The Chiang Kai-shek gang of Taiwan cannot remain in the United Nations. What we are dealing with, we repeat, is the expulsion of the usurper and the installation of the legitimate representative of the Chinese people.

We also warn against the U.S. Government's insistence on presenting the problem of the legitimate representation of China in the UN as an «important question» in order to impose a requirement of a two-thirds majority of members present and voting. The admission of the People's Republic of China to the United Nations is, in fact, an important question for the entire world, but not for the machinery of the United Nations, where it must constitute a mere question of procedure. In this way justice will be done. Almost as important as attaining justice, however, would be the demonstration, once and for all, that this august Assembly has eyes to see, ears to hear, tongues to speak with and sound criteria for making its decisions. The proliferation of nuclear weapons among the member states of NATO, and especially the possession of these devices of mass destruction by the Federal Republic of Germany, would make the possibility of an agreement on disarmament even more remote, and linked to such an agreement is the problem of the peaceful reunification of Germany. So long as there is no clear understanding, the existence of two Germanies must be recognized: that of the German Democratic Republic and the Federal Republic. The German problem can be solved only with the direct participation in negotiations of the German Democratic Republic with full rights. We shall only touch on the questions of economic development and international trade that are broadly represented in the agenda. In this very year of 1964 the Geneva conference was held at which a multitude of matters related to these aspects of international relations were dealt with. The warnings and forecasts of our delegation were fully confirmed, to the misfortune of the economically dependent countries.

We wish only to point out that insofar as Cuba is concerned, the United States of America has not implemented the explicit recommendations of that conference, and recently the U.S. Government also prohibited the sale of medicines to Cuba. By doing so it divested itself, once and for all, of the mask of humanitarianism with which it attempted to disguise the aggressive nature of its blockade against the people of Cuba.

Furthermore, we state once more that the scars left by colonialism that impede the development of the peoples are expressed not only in political relations. The so-called deterioration of the terms of trade is nothing but the result of the unequal exchange between countries producing raw materials and industrial countries, which dominate markets and impose the illusory justice of equal exchange of values.

So long as the economically dependent peoples do not free themselves from the capitalist markets and, in a firm bloc with the socialist countries, impose new relations between the exploited and the exploiters, there will be no solid economic development. In certain cases there will be retrogression, in which the weak countries will fall under the political domination of the imperialists and colonialists.

Finally, distinguished delegates, it must be made clear that in the area of the Caribbean, maneuvers and preparations for aggression against Cuba are taking place, on the coasts of Nicaragua above all, in Costa Rica as well, in the Panama Canal Zone, on Vieques Island in Puerto Rico, in Florida and possibly in other parts of U.S. territory and perhaps also in Honduras. In these places Cuban mercenaries are training, as well as mercenaries of other nationalities, with a purpose that cannot be the most peaceful one. After a big scandal, the government of Costa Rica — it is said — has ordered the elimination of all training camps of Cuban exiles in that country.

No-one knows whether this position is sincere, or whether it is a simple alibi because the mercenaries training there were about to commit some misdeed. We hope that full cognizance will be taken of the real existence of bases for aggression, which we denounced long ago, and that the world will ponder the international responsibility of the government of a country that authorizes and facilitates the training of mercenaries to attack Cuba. We should note that news of the training of mercenaries in different parts in the Caribbean and the participation of the U.S. Government in such acts is presented as completely natural in the newspapers in the United States. We know of no Latin American voice that has officially protested this. This shows the cynicism with which the U.S. Government moves its pawns.

The sharp foreign ministers of the OAS had eyes to see Cuban emblems and to find «irrefutable» proof in the weapons that the Yankees exhibited in Venezuela, but they do not see the preparations for aggression in the United States, just as they did not hear the voice of President Kennedy, who explicitly declared himself the aggressor against Cuba at Playa Girón [Bay of Pigs invasion of April 1961]. In some cases, it is a blindness provoked by the hatred against our revolution by the ruling classes of the Latin American countries. In others — and these are sadder and more deplorable — it is the product of the dazzling glitter of mammon.

As is well known, after the tremendous commotion of the so-called

Caribbean crisis, the United States undertook certain commitments with the Soviet Union. These culminated in the withdrawal of certain types of weapons that the continued acts of aggression of the United States — such as the mercenary attack at Playa Girón and threats of invasion against our homeland — had compelled us to install in Cuba as an act of legitimate and essential defense.

The United States, furthermore, tried to get the UN to inspect our territory. But we emphatically refuse, since Cuba does not recognize the right of the United States, or of anyone else in the world, to determine the type of weapons Cuba may have within its borders.

In this connection, we would abide only by multilateral agreements, with equal obligations for all the parties concerned. As Fidel Castro has said: «So long as the concept of sovereignty exists as the prerogative of nations and of independent peoples, as a right of all peoples, we will not accept the exclusion of our people from that right. So long as the world is governed by these principles, so long as the world is governed by those concepts that have universal validity because they are universally accepted and recognized by the peoples, we will not accept the attempt to deprive us of any of those rights, and we will renounce none of those rights.» The Secretary-General of the United Nations, U Thant, understood our reasons. Nevertheless, the United States attempted to establish a new prerogative, an arbitrary and illegal one: that of violating the airspace of a small country. Thus, we see flying over our country U-2 aircraft and other types of spy planes that, with complete impunity, fly over our airspace. We have made all the necessary warnings for the violations of our airspace to cease, as well as for a halt to the provocations of the U.S. Navy against our sentry posts in the zone of Guantánamo, the buzzing by aircraft of our ships or the ships of other nationalities in international waters, the pirate attacks against ships sailing under different flags, and the infiltration of spies, saboteurs and weapons onto our island.

We want to build socialism. We have declared that we are supporters of those who strive for peace. We have declared ourselves to be within the group of nonaligned countries, although we are Marxist-Leninists, because the nonaligned countries, like ourselves, fight imperialism. We want peace. We want to build a better life for our people. That is why we avoid, insofar as possible, falling into the provocations manufactured by the Yankees. But we know the mentality of those who govern them. They want to make us pay a very high price for that peace. We reply that the price cannot go beyond the bounds of dignity.

And Cuba reaffirms once again the right to maintain on its territory the weapons it deems appropriate, and its refusal to recognize the right of any power on earth — no matter how powerful — to violate our soil, our territorial waters, or our airspace.

If in any assembly Cuba assumes obligations of a collective nature, it will fulfill them to the letter. So long as this does not happen, Cuba maintains all its rights, just as any other nation. In the face of the demands of imperialism, our prime minister laid out the five points necessary for the existence of a secure peace in the Caribbean. They are:

1. A halt to the economic blockade and all economic and trade pressures by the United States, in all parts of the world, against our country.

2. A halt to all subversive activities, launching and landing of weap- ons and explosives by air and sea, organization of mercenary invasions, infiltration of spies and saboteurs, acts all carried out from the territory of the United States and some accomplice countries.

3. A halt to pirate attacks carried out from existing bases in the United States and Puerto Rico.

4. A halt to all the violations of our airspace and our territorial waters by U.S. aircraft and warships.

5. Withdrawal from the Guantánamo naval base and return of the Cuban territory occupied by the United States.»

None of these elementary demands has been met, and our forces are still being provoked from the naval base at Guantánamo. That base has become a nest of thieves and a launching pad for them into our territory. We would tire this Assembly were we to give a detailed account of the large number of provocations of all kinds. Suffice it to say that including the first days of December, the number amounts to 1,323 in 1964 alone. The list covers minor provocations such as violation of the boundary line, launching of objects from the territory controlled by the United States, the commission of acts of sexual exhibitionism by U.S. personnel of both sexes, and verbal insults. It includes others that are more serious, such as shooting off small caliber weapons, aiming weapons at our territory, and offenses against our national flag. Extremely serious provocations include those of crossing the boundary line and starting fires in installations on the Cuban side, as well as rifle fire. There have been 78 rifle shots this year, with the sorrowful toll of one death: that of Ramón López Peña, a soldier, killed by two shots fired from the U.S. post three and a half kilometers from the coast on the northern boundary. This extremely grave provocation took place at 7:07 p.m. on July 19, 1964, and the prime minister of our government publicly stated on July 26 that if the event were to recur he would give orders for our troops to repel the aggression. At the same time orders were given for the withdrawal of the forward line of Cuban forces to positions farther away from the boundary line and construction of the necessary fortified positions. One thousand three hundred and twenty-three provocations in 340 days amount to approximately four per day. Only a perfectly disciplined army with a morale such as ours could resist so many hostile acts without losing its self-control.

Forty-seven countries meeting at the Second Conference of Heads of State or Government of Nonaligned Countries in Cairo unanimously agreed:

Noting with concern that foreign military bases are in practice a means of bringing pressure on nations and retarding their emancipation and development, based on their own ideological, political, economic and cultural ideas, the conference declares its unreserved support to the countries that are seeking to secure the elimination of foreign bases from their territory and calls upon all states maintaining troops and bases in other countries to remove them immediately. The conference considers that the maintenance at Guantánamo (Cuba) of a military base of the United States of America, in defiance of the will of the government and people of Cuba and in defiance of the provisions embodied in the declaration of the Belgrade conference, constitutes a violation of Cuba's sovereignty and territorial integrity.

Noting that the Cuban Government expresses its readiness to settle its dispute over the base at Guantánamo with the United States of America on an equal footing, the conference urges the U.S. Government to open negotiations with the Cuban Government to evacuate their base.

The government of the United States has not responded to this request of the Cairo conference and is attempting to maintain indefinitely by force its occupation of a piece of our territory, from which it carries out acts of aggression such as those detailed earlier.

The Organization of American States — which the people also call the U.S.

Ministry of Colonies — condemned us «energetically,» even though it had just excluded us from its midst, ordering its members to break off diplomatic and trade relations with Cuba. The OAS authorized aggression against our country at any time and under any pretext, violating the most fundamental international laws, completely disregarding the United Nations. Uruguay, Bolivia, Chile and México opposed that measure, and the government of the United States of México refused to comply with the sanctions that had been approved. Since then we have had no relations with any Latin American countries except México, and this fulfills one of the necessary conditions for direct aggression by imperialism.

We want to make clear once again that our concern for Latin America is based on the ties that unite us: the language we speak, the culture we maintain, and the common master we had. We have no other reason for desiring the liberation of Latin America from the U.S. colonial yoke. If any of the Latin American countries here decide to reestablish relations with Cuba, we would be willing to do so on the basis of equality, and without viewing that recognition of Cuba as a free country in the world to be a gift to our government. We won that recognition with our blood in the days of the liberation struggle. We acquired it with our blood in the defense of our shores against the Yankee invasion.

Although we reject any accusations against us of interference in the internal affairs of other countries, we cannot deny that we sympathize with those people who strive for their freedom. We must fulfill the obligation of our government and people to state clearly and categorically to the world that we morally support and stand in solidarity with peoples who struggle anywhere in the world to make a reality of the rights of full sovereignty proclaimed in the UN Charter.

It is the United States that intervenes. It has done so historically in Latin America. Since the end of the last century Cuba has experienced this truth; but it has been experienced, too, by Venezuela, Nicaragua, Central America in general, México, Haiti and the Dominican Republic. In recent years, apart from our people, Panama has experienced direct aggression, where the marines in the Canal Zone opened fire in cold blood against the defenseless people; the Dominican Republic, whose coast was violated by the Yankee fleet to avoid an outbreak of the just fury of the people after the death of Trujillo; and Colombia, whose capital was taken by assault as a result of a rebellion provoked by the assassination of Gaitán. Covert interventions are carried out through military missions that participate in internal repression, organizing forces designed for that purpose in many countries, and also in coups d'état, which have been repeated so frequently on the Latin American continent during recent years. Concretely, U.S. forces intervened in the repression of the peoples of Venezuela, Colombia and Guatemala, who fought with weapons for their freedom. In Venezuela, not only do U.S. forces advise the army and the police, but they also direct acts of genocide carried out from the air against the peasant population in vast insurgent areas. And the Yankee companies operating there exert pressures of every kind to increase direct interference. The imperialists are preparing to repress the peoples of the Americas and are establishing an International of Crime.

The United States intervenes in Latin America invoking the defense of free institutions. The time will come when this Assembly will acquire greater maturity and demand of the U.S. Government guarantees for the life of the blacks and Latin Americans who live in that country, most of them U.S. citizens by origin or adoption.

Those who kill their own children and discriminate daily against them because of the color of their skin; those who let the murderers of blacks remain free, protecting them, and furthermore punishing the black population because they demand their legitimate rights as free men — how can those who do this consider themselves guardians of freedom? We understand that today the Assembly is not in a position to ask for explanations of these acts. It must be clearly established, however, that the government of the United States is not the champion of freedom, but rather the perpetrator of exploitation and oppression against the peoples of the world and against a large part of its own population.

To the ambiguous language with which some delegates have described the case of Cuba and the OAS, we reply with clear-cut words and we proclaim that the peoples of Latin America will make those servile, sell-out governments pay for their treason.

Cuba, distinguished delegates, a free and sovereign state with no chains binding it to anyone, with no foreign investments on its territory, with no proconsuls directing its policy, can speak with its head held high in this Assembly and can demonstrate the justice of the phrase by which it has been baptized: «Free Territory of the Americas.» Our example will bear fruit in the continent, as it is already doing to a certain extent in Guatemala, Colombia and Venezuela.

There is no small enemy nor insignificant force, because no longer are there isolated peoples. As the Second Declaration of Havana states:

No nation in Latin America is weak — because each forms part of a family of 200 million brothers, who suffer the same miseries, who harbor the same sentiments, who have the same enemy, who dream about the same better future, and who count upon the solidarity of all honest men and women throughout the world...

This epic before us is going to be written by the hungry Indian masses, the peasants without land, the exploited workers. It is going to be written by the progressive masses, the honest and brilliant intellectuals, who so greatly abound in our suffering Latin American lands. Struggles of masses and ideas. An epic that will be carried forward by our peoples, mistreated and scorned by imperialism; our people, unreckoned with until today, who are now beginning to shake off their slumber. Imperialism considered us a weak and submissive flock; and now it begins to be terrified of that flock; a gigantic flock of 200 million Latin Americans in whom Yankee monopoly capitalism now sees its gravediggers...

But now from one end of the continent to the other they are signaling with clarity that the hour has come — the hour of their vindication. Now this anonymous mass, this America of color, somber, taciturn America, which all over the continent sings with the same sadness and disillusionment, now this mass is beginning to enter definitively into its own history, is beginning to write it with its own blood, is beginning to suffer and die for it.

Because now in the mountains and fields of America, on its flatlands and in its jungles, in the wilderness or in the traffic of cities, on the banks of its great oceans or rivers, this world is beginning to tremble. Anxious hands are stretched forth, ready to die for what is theirs, to win those rights that were laughed at by one and all for 500 years. Yes, now history will have to take the poor of America into account, the exploited and spurned of America, who have decided to begin writing their history for themselves for all time. Already they can be seen on the roads, on foot, day after day, in an endless march of hundreds of kilometers to the governmental «eminences,» there to obtain their rights.

Already they can be seen armed with stones, sticks, machetes, in one direction and another, each day, occupying lands, sinking hooks into the land that belongs to them and defending it with their lives. They can be seen carrying signs, slogans, flags; letting them flap in the mountain or prairie winds. And the wave of anger, of demands for justice, of claims for rights trampled underfoot, which is beginning to sweep the lands of Latin America, will not stop. That wave will swell with every passing day. For that wave is composed of the greatest number, the majorities in every respect, those whose labor amasses wealth and turns the wheels of history. Now they are awakening from the long, brutalizing sleep to which they had been subjected.

For this great mass of humanity has said, «Enough!» and has begun to march. And their march of giants will not be halted until they conquer true independence — for which they have vainly died more than once. Today, however, those who die will die like the Cubans at Playa Girón. They will die for their own true and never-to-be-surrendered independence.

All this, distinguished delegates, this new will of a whole continent, of Latin America, is made manifest in the cry proclaimed daily by our masses as the irrefutable expression of their decision to fight and to paralyze the armed hand of the invader. It is a cry that has the understanding and support of all the peoples of the world and especially of the socialist camp, headed by the Soviet Union.

That cry is: **Patria o muerte!** (Homeland or Death!)

2. **Speech in the General Assembly of the United Nations in the exercise of his right to reply.**

I ask your indulgence for having to occupy this lectern once again. I do so making use of my right to reply. Naturally, although we are not especially interested in it, this could be called a counter-reply, and we could go on extending counter-replies ad infinitum. We will not reply one by one the statements made by the delegates that impugned Cuba's intervention, and we do so in the spirit in which each one of them did it, approximately.

I will begin by answering the delegate from Costa Rica, who lamented that Cuba has allowed itself to be carried away by some false news from a sensationalist press, declaring the his Government immediately took some inspection measures when the free press of Costa Rica, very different from the slave press in Cuba, made several denunciations. Perhaps the delegate from Costa Rica is correct. We cannot make absolute statements based on reports by the Imperialist press, especially from the United States made repeatedly to Cuban counter-revolutionaries. But if Artime was the chief of the failed Bay of Pigs invasion, he was with some sort of intermediary, because he was a chief until he reached the Cuban coast when he suffered the first casualties, returning to the United States. In the meantime, as with the majority of the members of the «heroic freedom expedition» he was «a cook or a nurse» because that is the way in which they got to Cuba after being in jail, according to their own statements, all these «liberators» of Cuba. Artime, who now is once again a chief, expressed his displeasure at the accusation. What is the accusation? Of smuggling whiskey, because in his bases in Costa Rica and Nicaragua, according to him, there is no whiskey smuggling: «there is training for revolutionaries to free Cuba.» These statements have been made to news agencies and they have traveled the world. In Costa Rica this has been denounced repeatedly. Patriotic Costa Ricans have reported the existence of these bases in the area of Tortugueras and nearby areas, and the Government of Costa Rica should know very well if this is true or not. We have absolute certainty about these reports, as we are also sure that Mr. Artime, among his multiple «revolutionary» activities has had time to smuggle whiskey, because these are natural things for this type of liberators that the Government of Costa Rica protects, even if only half-heartedly. We maintain, once and a thousand times, that revolutions are not exported. Revolutions are born in the midst of the people. Revolutions are engendered by the exploitation that governments —such as the ones of Costa Rica, Nicaragua, Panama or Venezuela— exert on their people. Later these liberation movements can be helped or not; especially they can be given moral backing. But the truth is that revolutions cannot be exported. We say so not as a justification in this Assembly; we say it simply as an expression of a scientific fact known for many years. That is why we would do wrong if we tried to export revolutions and least of all, naturally, to Costa Rica, where truth be told there is a regime in which we have absolutely no communion of any type, and is one that doesn't distinguish itself in the Americas for its

indiscriminate direct oppression against its people. With respect to
Nicaragua, we would like to say to its representative, although I didn't
exactly understand his argument regarding accents —I believe he was
referring to Cuba, and Argentina, and perhaps the Soviet Union— I trust
that in any case the representative of Nicaragua has not found a U.S.
accent in my speech because that would be dangerous. In fact, it is
possible that speaking with an Argentine accent may have escaped me. I
was born in Argentina; that is not a secret to anyone. I am Cuban and I
am also Argentine, and if the very illustrious gentlemen of Latin
America don't get offended, I feel as much as patriot of Latin America, of
any country in Latin America, as anyone, and, at the time when it may be
necessary, I would be ready to exchange my life for the liberation of any
of the countries of Latin America, without asking anything from anyone,
without demanding anything, without exploiting anyone. And thus is
my state of mind, this transitory representative to this Assembly is not
here alone. The entire Cuban people are so disposed. The entire Cuban
people throb each time an injustice is committed, not only in the Americas but in the whole world. We can say what we have said so many times
about the marvelous apothegm of Martí that a true man should feel in
the cheek the blow struck on any man's cheek. This, the entire people of
Cuba feel, yes gentlemen. In case the gentleman representative from
Nicaragua wants to make a small revision in his geographical map or if
he wants to make a visual inspection of places of difficult access, he can
go to Puerto Cabezas –where I believe he will not deny a part, or a great
part, of the Bay of Pigs expedition departed –from Blue Fields and
Monkey Point, which I believe should be called Punto Mono, and I don't
know by what strange historical accident being in Nicaragua is it called
Monkey Point. There he may find some counter-revolutionaries or
Cuban revolutionaries, like you prefer to call them, gentlemen representatives of Nicaragua. There are all types. There is also enough whiskey, I
don't know if smuggled or if directly imported. We know of the existence
of these bases. And, naturally, we are not going to demand that the OAS
investigate if they are there or not. We know of the selective blindness of
the OAS well enough to ask for such an absurdity. They say that we have
acknowledged having atomic weapons. There is no such thing. I believe
it must have been a small error on the part of the representative from
Nicaragua. We have only defended our right to have the weapons that

we are able to procure for our defense, and we have denied the right of any country to determine what type of arms we are going to have. The gentleman representative of Panama, who has had the kindness of nicknaming me Che, as the Cuban people call me, began by talking about the Mexican Revolution. The delegation of Cuba was talking about the U.S. massacre against the people of Panama and the delegation from Panamá began by talking about the Mexican Revolution, and went on in this same style, without mentioning at all the American massacre that led the Government of Panama to break relations with the United States. Perhaps in the language of surrender politics, this is called a tactic; in revolutionary language, this, gentlemen, is called abjection, spelled out. He referred to the invasion of 1959. A group of adventurers, led by a salon bearded one, who had never been to the Sierra Maestra, and who is now in Miami, or in some base somewhere, was able to recruit a group of boys to undertake that adventure. Officials of the Cuban Government worked jointly with those of the Panamanian Government to finish that. It is true that they left from a Cuban port, and it is also true that we discussed it in friendly terms then. Of all the speeches here against the Cuban delegation, the one that seems inexcusable in every sense is the one by the delegation of Panama. We didn't have the very least intention of offending her nor of offending the Government of Panama. We wanted to defend the people of Panama with a denunciation before the United Nations, given that its Government doesn't have the courage or the dignity to pose these matters with their proper names. We didn't want to offend the Government of Panama nor did we want to defend it. For the people of Panama, our fraternal people, goes our sympathy and we will try to defend them with our denunciation. Among the statements made by the representatives of Panama, there is something very interesting. He says that, despite Cuban bravado, the base is still there. In the intervention that should still be fresh in the memory of the representatives, it must be recognized that we have denounced 1300 provocations of all kinds from trivial ones to shooting with guns. We have explained how we don't want to fall for provocations because we know the consequences that they can have for our people; we have posed the issue of the base in Guantánamo in all international meetings and we have always claimed the right of the Cuban people to recuperate this base by peaceful means. We have not used bravado, because we don't do that, mister representative of Panama, because men like us, who are ready to die, who lead our entire people, we are ready to die to defend our cause, so we don't rely on bravado. We didn't speak with bravado in the Bay of Pigs; we didn't issue bravado during the Missile Crisis, when the whole people were facing the atomic mushroom with which the Americans were threatening our Island, and the whole people marched to the trenches, marched on the factories, to increase production. There was not a step back, not one complaint, and thousands and thousands of people who didn't belong to our militias voluntarily joined them at the time when American Imperialism was threatening to drop a bomb or several atomic bombs or carry out an atomic attack on Cuba. That is our country. And such a country, whose leaders and whose people —I can say so with my head high— are not afraid of death whatsoever, know well the responsibility for its actions, so we never issue bravado. What is true is that we fight to the death, mister representative of Panama, if necessary, and it will fight to the death, with its Government, the whole people of Cuba is attacked. The representative of Colombia states, all in all polite —and I also have to change my tone of voice— that there were inaccurate statements: one, the Yankee invasion of 1948 after the assassination of Jorge Eliecer Gaitán; and from the tone of voice of the representative of Colombia, I can tell that he feels strongly about that death: that his is deeply sorrowful. We referred, in our speech, to a previous intervention which, perhaps, the representative from Colombia forgot about: the American intervention that led to the secession of Panama. Then he spoke that there are no liberation troops in Colombia, as there is nothing to liberate. In Colombia, where one speaks so naturally about representative democracy and there are only two political parties that share power half and half for years, following a fantasy democracy, the Colombian oligarchy has reached the summum of democracy, we could say. It is divided between liberals and conservatives and then conservatives and liberals; four years for one and four for the other. Nothing changes. These are the democracies of elections; these are the representative democracies that he defends, probably with all his enthusiasm, the representative of Colombia, in that country where it is said that there have been 200,000 to 300,000 deaths since the civil war that ignited Colombia after Gaitán's death. And, however, he says there is nothing to liberate. There will be nothing to avenge either; there will not be thousands of deaths to avenge; there would not have been armies massacring their people and it will not be that same army that has been massacring their people since the year 1948. What is there has been somewhat changed, or their generals are different, or their commanders are different or obey a different class than the one that massacred the people during four long years of struggle and continued to massacre off and on for several more years. And he says that there is nothing to liberate. Doesn't the representative of Colombia recall that in Marquetalia there are forces that eleven Colombian newspapers have called the «Independent Republic of Marquetalia» and that one of its leaders has gotten the nickname of Tiro Fijo (Sure Shot) to try to turn him into a vulgar bandit? And doesn't he know that large operations were done there with 16,000 men from the Colombian army, advised by the U.S. military, and utilizing a series of elements such as helicopters, and that probably — although I cannot vouch for it— with airplanes, also from the U.S. Army? It seems that the representative from Colombia has bad information as he is away from his country or his memory is a bit deficient. Additionally, the representative of Colombia spoke freely that if Cuba had continued to be in the orbit of the American states things would be different. We don't exactly know what he was talking about referring to an orbit; but orbits are for satellites and we are not satellites. We are in no orbit, we are off the orbit. Naturally, had we made here a mellifluous speech several pages long, naturally in a much finer Castilian, much more substantial and adjectival, and if we had talked about the beauty of the Inter-American system, and of our firm and unmovable defense of the free world directed by the center of the orbit, which everyone knows who it is. I don't need to mention it. The representative from Venezuela also employed a moderate tone, although emphatic. He spoke that accusations of genocide are infamous and that it was really incredible for the Cuban government to concern itself with these matters in Venezuela given the repression it has against its own people. We have to say something here, which is a known truth, which we have always expressed before the world: firing squads, yes, we have shot people; we have firing squads and will continue to have firing squads as long as needed. Our fight is a fight to the death. We know what would be the result of a lost battle and the worms have to know the meaning of the outcome of the battle lost today in Cuba. We live under these conditions imposed by

U.S. Imperialism. But this is true: we don't commit murders, as are being committed right now by the Venezuelan police with I believe the name of Digepol, if I'm not misinformed. This police force is conducting a series of barbaric acts, shootings, that is, murders, to later throw away the corpses in different places. This has happened for example against the person, for example of students, etc. The free press in Venezuela has been suspended several times in the last few months for providing a series of reports of this type. Venezuelan military airplanes with Yankee advice, yes, bombard large peasant areas, they kill peasants; yes, the popular rebellion is growing in Venezuela, and yes, we will see the results after some time.

The gentleman representative from Venezuela is incensed. I recall the indignation of the gentlemen representatives of Venezuela when the Cuban delegation in Punta del Este read secret reports from a spokesperson of the United States of America, which they naturally made available to us, indirectly, of course. At that time we read before the assembly in Punta del Este the opinion that the representatives of the United States had about the Venezuelan Government. They were announcing something very interesting --pardon the lack of accuracy as I cannot cite it verbatim-- but it went somewhat like this «Either these people change or they will all face the firing squad.» Firing squads is the way in which they want to portray the Cuban Revolution; firing squads. The members of the U.S. Embassy were announcing in irrefutable documents that this was the destiny of the Venezuelan oligarchy if they didn't change their ways, and so they were accusing it of larceny, and so, all types of similarly terrible accusations were being made. The Venezuelan delegation of course got very incensed; but it was not indignation against the United States, its rage was against the Cuban delegation which had the courtesy of reading to them the opinions that the U.S. had about their Government, and their people as well. Yes, the only reply made to all this was that Mr. Moscoso, who kindly ceded some of these documents indirectly, had to change jobs. We remind this to the gentleman representative of Venezuela because revolutions are not exported; revolutions act, and the Venezuelan revolution will act in its time, and those that don't have their airplanes ready —as happened in Cuba— to flee to Miami, or to other places, will have to face there whatever the Venezuelan people decide. Don't blame other people, other governments, for what might happen there. I want to recommend to the gentleman representative of Venezuela that if he is interested, he should read some of the very interesting opinions about what is guerrilla warfare and how to fight it, that some very intelligent members of COPEI have written and published in the press of your country...He will see that with bombs and murders is not the way to fight against a people in rebellion. Precisely, this is what turns people into more revolutionaries. We know it well. It is not right to as a favor show a declared enemy counter-guerrilla strategy, but we do so as we know that their blindness is such that they will not follow it. Mr. Stevenson has left. Unfortunately he is not present. We understand perfectly well why Mr. Stevenson is not present. We have heard once again his relevant and serious statements, worthy of an intellectual of his stature. Similarly emphatic, relevant and serious declarations were made during the first commission, April 15, 1961, during session 1,149, precisely the day when pirate U.S. aircraft with Cuban insignias —leaving from Puerto Cabezas, as far as I can recall, from Nicaragua, or perhaps from Guatemala, it's not well documented— bombarded Cuban airports almost reducing to zero our air force. The airplanes, after conducting their «feat» landed in the United States. Facing our denunciation, Mr. Stevenson said some very interesting things. Please forgive the length of my appearance, but I believe it is deserving to remember once again the relevant phrases of such a distinguished intellectual as Mr. Stevenson, spoken hardly four or five days before Mr. Kennedy calmly stated, facing the world, that he assumed all responsibility for the events that had occurred in Cuba. This is, I believe, a simple review, since given the short time that we had we have not been able to compile accurate transcripts of each of the meetings. They go like this: «The accusations formulated against the United States by the representative from Cuba, respecting bombardments, which as he reports, have been conducted against the airports of Havana and Santiago, and on the headquarters of the Cuban Air Force in San Antonio de los Baños, are totally unfounded.» And Mr. Stevenson categorically rejected them. «As was declared by the President of the United States, the U.S. armed forces would not intervene under any circumstance in Cuba, and the United States will do all it can in order for no American to participate in any action against Cuba.» A little more than a year later we had the courtesy of returning to them the corpse of a pilot who crashed in Cuban territory. Not that of Major

Anderson; another one of that time. «Regarding the events that are supposed to have happened this morning and yesterday, the United States will study the petitions for political asylum in conformity with normal processes.» They were going to provide political asylum to the people they had sent. «Whoever believes in freedom and seeks asylum against tyranny and oppression will always find understanding and a favorable reception on the part of the American people and the Government of the United States.» And so Mr. Stevenson goes on in his long peroration. Two days later, the members of Brigade 2506 land in the Bay of Pigs, surely known for their heroism in the annals of American history. Two days later the heroic brigade surrenders without hardly losing a man, and then begins that tourney —that some of you are familiar with— of men dressed with the uniforms of worms that the U.S. Army has, saying they were cooks and nurses or that they had come as sailors in that expedition. It was then that President Kennedy had a dignified gesture. He didn't try to go on with a false policy that nobody believed and he said clearly that he was taking responsibility for all that had happened in Cuba. He took responsibility, yes; but the Organization of American States didn't hold him accountable nor did it demand any responsibility of any sort that we can remember. It was a responsibility before its own history, before the history of the United States, because the Organization of American States was in its orbit. It didn't have the time to take care of these matters. I thank Mr. Stevenson for his historic reference to my long life as a Communist and revolutionary that culminated in Cuba. As usual, U.S. agencies, not only in news, but also in espionage, confuse things. My revolutionary history is short and really starts with the Granma, and follows to this day. I didn't belong to the Communist Party until now that I am in Cuba and we can proclaim before this Assembly that Marxist-Leninism is what the Cuban Revolution follows as a theory of action. The important thing is not personal references; what is important is that Mr. Stevenson once again says that there is no violation of laws, that the airplanes don't depart from here, as there are also no ships, of course; that the pirate attacks come out of nowhere, that everything comes out of nowhere. He makes use of the same voice, the same assuredness, the same intellectual and firm accent that he used in 1961 to sustain, emphatically, that those Cuban airplanes had left from Cuban territory and that they were manned by political exiles, before being denied. Naturally, I understand, once again, how my distinguished colleague, Mr. Stevenson, decided to depart from this Assembly. The United States believes it can undertake surveillance flights because they were approved by the Organization of American States. Who is the Organization of American States to approve surveillance flights over the territory of a country? What is the role played by the United Nations? What is the purpose of this Organization if our destiny is going to depend on the orbit, so well defined by the gentleman representative of Colombia, of the Organization of American States?

This is a very serious and important question that needs to be asked before this Assembly. Because we, a small country, cannot accept, in any fashion, the right of a big country to violate our air space; and not for sure with the novel idea that its actions are backed by the legality of the Organization of American States, the same one that expelled us from its midst and to which no connecting link exists with us. The statements from the representative of the United States are very serious. I only want to say two things. I am not thinking of taking up all the time of the Assembly with replies and counter-replies. The gentleman representative of the United States says that Cuba blames its economic disaster on the embargo, when it is a problem caused by bad Government management. When none of this had happened, when the first nationalistic laws began in Cuba, the United States began to take repressive economic actions such as the unilateral suppression, without distinction, of the sugar quota, which we traditionally sold to the American market. As well, they refused to refine our oil that we had bought from the Soviet Union which was our legitimate right under all manner of laws. I will not repeat the long history of economic aggressions that the United States has done. I will say that, despite these aggressions, with the fraternal aid of Socialist countries, especially the Soviet Union, we have gone on and we will continue to go on; that although we condemn the economic embargo it will not stop us, and regardless of what happens, we will continue to be a small headache when we arrive in this Assembly or any other, to call things by their name and to call out the representatives of the United States, gendarmes of repression in the whole world. And lastly, there was an embargo of medicines against Cuba. But if this is not so, our Government will place in the next few months an order for medicines here in the United States, and will send a telegram to Mr.

Stevenson, which our representative will read before the commission or wherever its convenient, so he will know well if the imputations that Cuba makes are true or not. In any case, up to now they have been. The last time we tried to buy medicines in the amount of $1,500,000, medicines that are not manufactured in Cuba and that are needed exclusively to save lives, the U.S. government intervened and voided the sale. Recently, the President of Bolivia told our delegates, with tears in his eyes, that he had to break up with Cuba because the United States were forcing him to do it.

That is how they bid farewell to our delegates in La Paz. I cannot affirm that his statement of the President of Bolivia is true. What is true is that we told him that this transaction with the enemy was not worthwhile, because he was already condemned. The President of Bolivia, with whom we have no relationship, with whose Government we have only maintained relations as should be maintained with all the peoples of the Americas, has been overthrown by a military coup d'état. Now a Ruling Junta has been established there. At any rate, for people like this, who don't know how to fall with dignity, it is worthwhile to recall what I believe the mother of the last Caliph of Granada told her son who was crying at losing his city: «You do well to cry like a woman what you didn't know how to defend like a man.»

Che's farewell letter to Fidel

«Year of Agriculture»

Havana

Fidel:

At this moment I remember many things: when I met you in Maria Antonia's house, when you proposed I should come along, all the tensions involved in the preparations. One day they came by and asked who should be notified in case of death, and the real possibility of it struck us all. Later we knew it was true, that in a revolution one wins or dies (if it is a real one). Many comrades fell along the way to victory.

Today everything has a less dramatic tone, because we are more mature, but the event repeats itself. I feel that I have fulfilled the part of my duty that tied me to the Cuban revolution in its territory, and I say farewell to you, to the comrades, to your people, who now are mine.

I formally resign my positions in the leadership of the party, my post as minister, my rank of commander, and my Cuban citizenship. Nothing legal binds me to Cuba. The only ties are of another nature — those that cannot be broken as can appointments to posts.

Reviewing my past life, I believe I have worked with sufficient integrity and dedication to consolidate the revolutionary triumph. My only serious failing was not having had more confidence in you from the first moments in the Sierra Maestra, and not having understood quickly enough your qualities as a leader and a revolutionary.

I have lived magnificent days, and at your side I felt the pride of belonging to our people in the brilliant yet sad days of the Caribbean [Missile] crisis. Seldom has a statesman been more brilliant as you were in those days. I am also proud of having followed you without hesitation, of having identified with your way of thinking and of seeing and appraising dangers and principles.

Other nations of the world summon my modest efforts of assistance. I can do that which is denied you due to your responsibility as the head of Cuba, and the time has come for us to part.

You should know that I do so with a mixture of joy and sorrow. I leave here the purest of my hopes as a builder and the dearest of those I hold dear. And I leave the people who received me as a son. That wounds a part of my spirit. I carry to new battlefronts the faith that you taught me, the revolutionary spirit of my people, the feeling of fulfilling the most sacred of duties: to fight against imperialism wherever it may be. This is a source of strength, and more than heals the deepest of wounds.

I state once more that I free Cuba from all responsibility, except that which stems from its example. If my final hour finds me under other skies, my last thought will be of these people and especially of you. I am grateful for your teaching and your example, to which I shall try to be faithful up to the final consequences of my acts.

I have always been identified with the foreign policy of our revolution, and I continue to be. Wherever I am, I will feel the responsibility of being a Cuban revolutionary, and I shall behave as such. I am not sorry that I leave nothing material to my wife and children; I am happy it is that way. I ask nothing for them, as the state will provide them with enough to live on and receive an education.

I would have many things to say to you and to our people, but I feel they are unnecessary. Words cannot express what I would like them to, and there is no point in scribbling pages.

Until victory forever, Homeland or Death!

A hug with all the revolutionary fervor,

Che

4. Poem by Che dedicated to his wife Aleida March «Against Wind and Tide» (Against All Odds)

This poem (against wind and tide) will carry my signature.

I give you six sonorous syllables,

a gaze that always carries (like a wounded bird), tenderness.

An anxiety of warm and deep water.

A dark office where the only light is the one coming from my verses.

A very used thimble for your boring nights,

a photograph of our children.

The most beautiful bullet of this pistol that is always with me,

the inerasable memory (always latent and deep) of the children,

that one day, you and I conceived,

and the piece of life that I've got left,

this I give (convinced and happy) to the Revolution.

Nothing that can unite us can have greater strength.

Poem by Che to Jesus of Nazareth

Inside Che's backpack were found —to the surprise of many— a text rewritten by Che a few days before his death or a poem by poet León Felipe dedicated to Christ, which goes as follows:

«Christ, I love you

Not because you came down from a star,

But because you revealed to me

That man has tears,

Grief,»

Keys to open the doors filled with light.

If... you taught me that man is God,

A poor God crucified like you.

And that one on you left at

Golgotha, the bad thief,
Is also a God.

6. Story written by Che at the death of his mother Celia

(This is the impacting testimonial written by Che in the Congo, after
   receiving the news from Osmany Cienfuegos about the possible death of
   Celia, his mother. Its date of writing is sometime after May 22, 1965).

THE STONE

He told me how they should say these things to a strong man, to a responsible man, and I was grateful. He didn't lie, worry or pain and I tried not
   to show either one or the other. It was so simple!
Besides, we had to wait for confirmation to be officially sad. I wondered if
   you could mourn a little. No, it shouldn't be, because the boss is impersonal; it's not that you are denying his right to feel, simply, he must not
   show his own feelings, his soldiers', perhaps.
- It was a family friend, they phoned him telling that she was really severe,
   but I went out that day.
-Severe, deathly?
- Yes.
- Don't stop letting me know about everything.
As soon as I know, there is no hope. I think.

The messenger of death had already left and I had no confirmation. Waiting
   was all that one was able to do. With the official notice I was going to
   decide whether or not to show my sadness. I was inclined to think I
   wasn't.
The morning sun was hitting hard after the rain. There was nothing strange
   about it, every day it rained and then the sun came out and pressed and
   expelled the moisture. In the afternoon, the brook would be crystalline
   again, but that day hadn't fallen much water in the mountains. It was
   almost normal.
- They were saying that the 20th of May will stop raining and there is not
   going to fall a single drop of water until October.
- They were saying... but they say so many things that are not true.

- Will the Nature be guided by the calendar? I did not care if nature is guided or not by the calendar.

Usually, I could say that I did not care anything about anything, nor this forced inactivity, or this idiotic, aimless war. Well, not aimless, only it was so vague, so diluted that it seemed unattainable, like a surreal hell where eternal punishment was tedium. And besides, I did care. Of course I cared.

We must find a way to break this, I thought. And it was easy to think, one could make a thousand plans, one more tempting than the other, then select the best, melt two or three in one, simplify it, put it on paper and deliver it. That was where everything ended and you had to start all over. A smarter bureaucracy than normal, instead of saving it, you made it disappear. My men said they smoked it, all pieces of paper can be smoked, if there is something inside. It was an advantage, I could change what I didn't like in the next plan. No one would notice. It seemed that it would continue to infinity.

I needed to smoke so I pulled the pipe. It was, as always, in my pocket. I did not lose my pipes, as the soldiers did. It was really important for me to have it. On the roads of smoke you can go back through any distance, I would say that you could even believe in your own plans and dream with the victory without it seeming a dream; just a steamy reality because of the distance and the mists that are always on the roads of smoke. A very good companion is the pipe. How could someone lose such a necessary thing? What brutes.

They were not brutes, they had activities and they were tired of activities. There's no need to think then. And what use is a pipe without thinking? But it's possible to dream. Yes, you can dream, but the pipe is important when you dream far away, towards a future in which its only way is smoke or to a past so distant that it is needed to use the same path. But the nearby longings are felt with an- other body part, they have vigorous feet and young sight, they do not need the help of smoke. The other soldiers lose their pipes because for them it was not essential, the essential things are not lost.

Would this man have something more? The chiffon handkerchief. That was different, she gave it to me because if they hurt me in the arm, it would be a loving sling. The difficulty was in use if they broke me carapace. Actually there was an easy solution, which I put in my head to pull up my jaw and I'll go with it to the grave. Loyal even in death. If I was left lying on a field or I was picked up by the others there wouldn't be any chiffon handkerchief, I would be decomposed between the weeds or They will exhibit me and perhaps I would appear in Life magazine with an agonic and desperate gaze fixed at the supreme moment of fear. Because one is afraid, why should one deny it?

Through the smoke, I walked my old ways and came to the inmost corners of my fears, always linked to death like that nothingness disturbing and inexplicable, as much as us, the Marxists-Leninists explain very well the death as the nothingness. And what is that nothingness? Nothing. It is impossible to find a more simple and convincing explanation. The Nothingness is nothing, shut your brain, put a black cloak, if you like, with a sky of distant stars, and that's the nothingness-nothing. Equivalent: infinite.

One survives in this species, in History, which is a mystified way of life in the species; in these acts, in those memories. Have you ever felt a shiver down the spine reading Maceo's machete charges: that's the life after the nothingness. The children, too. I would not want to survive with my children: they don't know me, I am a foreign body that sometimes disturbs their peace of mind, when It interposes between them and their mother.

I imagined my grown son and her, grizzled, telling him, reproachfully: your father would have never done such or such a thing. I felt inside of me, the son of my father, a tremendous rebellion. Me, son, I would not know whether it was true or not that my father hadn't done this or that bad thing, but I would feel humiliated, betrayed by the memory of me, father that they rubbed upon my face all the time. My son had to be a man, nothing more, better or worse, but a man. I thanked my father and his sweet, loose affection without examples. What about my mother? Poor old lady. Officially, I still had no right, so I had to wait for confirmation.

Like that, I was walking by my route of smoke when I was interrupted by a
soldier, who was joyful for being useful.

-Have you lost anything?

-Nothing- I said, associating it with another of my reverie.

-Think carefully.

I touched my pockets, all in order.

-Nothing.

-And this little stone? I saw it on your keychain.

-Ah, fuck.

Then the reproach hit me with savage force. You don't lose something necessary, vitally necessary. And, does anyone live if they are not necessary
themselves? Vegetatively yes, but not a moral being. At least, I don't
think so.

I even felt the dip in the memory and I saw myself searching in the pockets
with rigorous thoroughness, while the brook, brownish of mountainous
soil, hid my secret. The pipe, the pipe first. There it was. The papers or
handkerchief would have floated. The vaporizer, present; the feathers
here; the notebooks in its nylon lining, yes; the matchbox, also present,
all in order. The dip was dissolved.

I only carried two small memories to the fight, the chiffon handkerchief that
belonged to my wife and the keychain with the stone that belonged to
my mother. This is very cheap, ordinary; the stone stuck off the keychain
so I put it in my pocket.

Was I merciful or vengeful, or just impersonal like a boss, the brook? You
don't cry because it is not due or because you can't? Is there no right to
forget, even in the war? Is it necessary to put a male disguise on the ice?

What would I know?. I really do not know. I only know that I have a physical
need for my mother to appear so I'd recline my head on her lean lap
while she says to me, «my old man» with a dry, full tenderness and I'd
feel in my hair her clumsy hand, caressing me in leaps, like a string doll,
as if the tenderness was coming out of her eyes and voice, because the
broken conductors don't let it reach the extremities. And the hands
shake and palpate more than they caress, but the tenderness slips out
and surrounds them and it feels so good, so tiny and so strong. There's

no need to apologize, she understands everything, you know it when you hear that «my old man»...

- Is it strong? It also affects me; yesterday I almost fell when I was going to stand up. Seems like they don't let it dry well.

-It's a shit! I'm waiting for the order to see if they bring decent fine-cut tobacco. One has the right to smoke even a pipe, quiet and tasty right? ...

7. Note from Che in the Congo regarding the death of his mother

I only know that I have the physical need for my mother to show up and for me to recline my head on her slim lap, and for her to tell me «my old man» with a dry and full tenderness, and to feel in my hair her clumsy hand caressing me at times, like a wound-up doll, as if tenderness came out of her eyes and voice because the broken conductors don't make it reach her extremities. And her hands feel more than they caress, but tenderness spills over and surrounds her and one feels so good, so little, so strong. It is not necessary to ask for her forgiveness; she understands it all, one knows when one is listening to «my old man». Che Guevara.

8. Memorandum from the Cuban Central Intelligence 172. Memorandum from Director of Central Intelligence Agency - Helms

Washington, October 13, 1967

MEMORANDUM FOR

The Secretary of State

The Secretary of Defense

Mr. Walt W. Rostow

Assistant Secretary of State for Inter-American Affairs

SUBJECT

Statements by Ernesto "Che" Guevara Prior to His Execution in Bolivia

1. Further details have now been obtained from [less than 1 line of source text not declassified] who was on the scene in the small village of Higueras where Ernesto "Che" Guevara was taken after his capture on 8 October 1967 by the Bolivian Army's Second Ranger Battalion.

2. [less than 1 line of source text not declassified] attempted to interrogate Guevara on 9 October 1967 as soon as he got access to him at around 7 a.m. At that time "Che" Guevara was sitting on the floor in the corner of a small, dark schoolroom in Higueras [sic]. He had his hands over his face. His wrists and feet were tied. In front of him on the floor lay the corpses of two Cuban guerrillas. Guevara had a flesh wound in his leg, which was bandaged.

3. Guevara refused to be interrogated but permitted himself to be drawn into a conversation with [less than 1 line of source text not declassified] during which he made the following comments:

a. Cuban economic situation: Hunger in Cuba is the result of pressure by United States imperialism. Now Cuba has become self-sufficient in meat production and has almost reached the point where it will begin to export meat. Cuba is the only economically self-sufficient country in the Socialist world.

b. Camilo Cienfuegos: For many years the story has circulated that Fidel Castro Ruz had Cienfuegos, one of his foremost deputies, killed because his personal popularity presented a danger to Castro. Actually the death of Cienfuegos was an accident. Cienfuegos was in Oriente Province when he received a call to attend a general staff meeting in Havana. He left by plane and the theory was that the plane became lost in low-ceiling flying conditions, consumed all of its fuel, and crashed in the ocean, and no trace of him was ever found. Castro had loved Cienfuegos more than any of his lieutenants.

c. Fidel Castro Ruz: Castro had not been a Communist prior to the success of the Cuban Revolution. Castro's own statements on the subject are correct.

d. The Congo: American imperialism had not been the reason for his failure there but, rather, the Belgian mercenaries. He denied ever having several thousand troops in the Congo, as sometimes reported, but admitted having had "quite a few".

e. Treatment of Guerrilla Prisoners in Cuba: During the course of the Cuban Revolution and its aftermath, there had been only about 1,500 individuals killed, exclusive of armed encounters such as the Bay of Pigs. The Cuban Government, of course, executed all guerrilla leaders who invaded its territory. . . . (He stopped then with a quizzical look on his face and smiled as he recognized his own position on Bolivian soil.)

f. Future of the Guerrilla Movement in Bolivia: With his capture, the guerrilla movement had suffered an overwhelming setback in Bolivia, but he predicted a resurgence in the future. He insisted that his ideals would win in the end even though he was disappointed at the lack of response from the Bolivian campesinos. The guerrilla movement had failed partially because of Bolivian Government propaganda which claimed that the guerrillas represented a foreign invasion of Bolivian soil. In spite of the lack of popular response from the Bolivian campesinos, he had not planned an exfiltration route from Bolivia in case of failure. He had definitely decided to either fall or win in this effort.

4. According to [less than 1 line of source text not declassified] when Guevara, Simon Cuba, and Aniceto Reynaga Gordillo were captured on 8 October, the Bolivian Armed Forces Headquarters ordered that they be kept alive for a time. A telegraphic code was arranged between La Paz and Higueras with the numbers 500 representing Guevara, 600 meaning the phrase "keep alive" and 700 representing "execute". During the course of the discussion with Guevara, Simon Cuba and Aniceto Reynaga were detained in the next room of the school house. At one stage, a burst of shots was heard and [less than 1 line of source text not declassified] learned later that Simon Cuba had been executed. A little later a single shot was heard and it was learned afterward that Aniceto Reynaga had been killed. When the order came at 11:50 a.m. from La Paz to kill Guevara, the execution was delayed as long as possible. However, when the local commander was advised that a helicopter would arrive to recover the bodies at approximately 1:30 p.m., Guevara was executed with a burst of shots at 1:15 p.m. Guevara's last words were, "Tell my wife to remarry and tell Fidel Castro that the Revolution will again rise in the Americas." To his executioner he said, "Remember, you are killing a man."

5. At no time during the period he was under [less than 1 line of source text not declassified] observation did Guevara lose his composure.

/1/ Source: Johnson Library, National Security File, Country File, Bolivia, Vol. IV, Memoranda, January 1966-December 1968. Secret. Copies of this memorandum in CIA files indicate that it was drafted by Broe and [name not declassified] in the Western Hemisphere Division and approved by Karamessines. (Central Intelligence Agency, DDO/IMS, Operational Group, Job 78-06423A, U.S. Government-President).

BIBLIOGRAPHY

Alarcón Ramírez, (Benigno). *Memorias de un soldado cubano*, Tusquets Editores, S.A., 1997.

American Psychiatric Association. *Manual diagnóstico y estadístico de trastornos mentales*, 2008.

Arana Serrudo, Federico. *Che Guevara y otras intrigas*, Editorial Temas de Hoy, Bolivia, 2002.

Aveledo, Ramón Guillermo. *El Dictador*, Editorial Libros Marcados, 2008.

Benemelis, Juan F. *Castro, subversión y terrorismo en África*, Editorial San Martín, 1988.

Blasier, Cole. *The Hovering Giants*, University of Pittsburg Press, 1976.

Borrego, Orlando. *Che: el camino de fuego*, Ediciones Hombre Nuevo, Buenos Aires, 2001.

Cao Mendiguren, Andrés. *La verdadera República de Cuba*, Ediciones Universal, 2008.

Carrolton Press. *The Desclassified Document Catalogue*. Vol XXI no.2, 1995, File # 0649.

Castañeda, Jorge G. *La vida en rojo*, Alfaguara, 1997.

Castro, Juanita. *Fidel y Raúl, mis hermanos*, Santillana, USA, 2009.

Castro, Fidel. *La victoria estratégica,* PCC, Comité Central, 2010.

Castro, *Fidel La contraofensiva estratégica*, PCC, Comité Central, 2010.

Cerrato, Rafael. *Amanecer en la Higuera*, Alexandria Library, 2012.

Constenla, Julia. *Celia, la madre del Che*, Editorial Suramericana, 2004.

Cupull and González. *La CIA contra el Che*, Editora Política, 1996.

Debray, Regis. *Praised Be Our Lords*, Editions Gallimard, 1996.

Deutscher, Isaac. *La Revolución inconclusa*, Ediciones Era, 1967.

Dunkerley, James. *Warriors and Scribes: Essays on Latin American*, London, Verso, 2000.

Encinosa, Enrique G. *Escambray, la guerra olvidada*, Editorial SIBI, 1989.

Fernández León, Julio. *José A. Echeverría, vigencia y presencia*, Ediciones Universal, 2007.

Fernández Montes de Oca. *El Diario de Pacho*, Editorial Punto y Coma, 1987.

Figes, Orlando, *The Whisperers', Private Life in Stalin's Russia*, Picador, 2008

Franqui, Carlos. *Retrato de familia con Fidel*, Editores Seix Barral, 1981.

Friedl Zapata, José A. *Tania la Guerrillera*, Editorial SIBI, 2000.

Fuentes, Norberto. *The Autobiography of Fidel*, Norton Paperback, 2010.

Guedes, Emilio. *Cuba, la revolución que no fue*, Eriginal Books, 2013

Guevara, Ernesto. *El Diario del Che en Bolivia*, Siglo XXI Editores, 1968.

Guevara, Ernesto. *La guerra de guerrillas*, Editorial 21, 2003.

Guevara, Ernesto. *Pasajes de la Guerra Revolucionaria (Congo)*, Edit. Océano Sur, 2009.

Lee Anderson, John. *Che Guevara*, Grove Press, New York, 1997.

Lovett, Joan. *La curación trauma infantil DRMO*, Editorial Pardos Ibérica, 2000

Marsant, Joseph. *La séptima muerte del Che*, Plaza y Janés, 1979.

Mesa Lago, Carmelo. *Cuba en la era de Raúl Castro*, Editorial Colibrí, 2012.

Müller, Alberto. *Cuba: entre dos extremos*, Ediciones Universal, 1984.

O'Donnelll, Pacho. *Che*, Editorial Debolsillo, 2005.

Ortega, Luis. *Yo soy el Che*, Ediciones Espuela de Plata, 2009.

Malo de Molina, Gustavo. *Frank País: apuntes sobre un luchador clandestino*, Ed. Gente Nueva

Posse, Abel. *Los cuadernos de Praga*, Emecé Editores, 2007.

Ramonet, Ignacio. *Fidel Castro, biografía a dos voces*, Random House, 2006.

Ramos, Marco Antonio. *La Cuba de Castro y después*, Rojas Editores, 2007.

Rodríguez, Félix and Weisman, John. *Shadow Warrior*, NY, Simon & Schuster, 1989.

Rojo, Ricardo. *Mi amigo el Che*, Ediciones Debolsillo, 2006.

Ros, Enrique. *El clandestinaje y la lucha armada contra Castro*, Ediciones Universal, 2006

Ros, Enrique. *La aventura africana de Fidel Castro*, Ediciones Universal, 1999.

Ros, Enrique. *Fidel Castro y el gatillo alegre*, Ediciones Universal, 2003.

Ros, Enrique. E. *Guevara,Mito y Realidad*, Ediciones Universal, 2003/ pag.13

Rostow, Walter. *Walter Rostow to the President, Secret NSF*, LBJ Library, October 18, 1967.

Suchlicki, Jaime. *Breve historia de Cuba*, Ediciones Pureplay Press, 2006.

Tabio, Paco Ignacio. *Ernesto Guevara, también conocido como el Che*, Planeta, 1996.

Vargas Salinas, Mario. *Che: mito y realidad*, Editorial La Paz, 1988.

Vasile, Vicenzo and Cereghino, Mario. *Che Guevara*, Top Secret, Bompiani, 2006.

Villegas, Harry. *Pombo, un hombre de la guerrilla del Che*, Castilian Editions. 1996.
Weiss, Mitch and Maurer, Kevin. *Hunting Che*, Berkeley Edit. 2013.

Name index

A
Acevedo, Enrique
Acuña Nuñez, Vitalio, (alias Joaquín)
Adriazola, David, (alias Darío)
Alarcón Ramírez, Daniel (alias Benigno)
Alexeiv, Alexander
Almeida, Juan
Alonso, Aurelio
Álvarez Rom, Luis
Amaya, Zenteno
Aquino Quispe, Apolinar
Aragonés, Emilio
Arbenz, Jacobo;
Ascencio, Lázaro

B
Badelaire, Charles
Barrera, Quintana, Pastor
Barrientos, René
Batista, Fulgencio
Bazán, Orlando
Bazán, Raúl (alias Camba)
Béjar, Hector
Ben Bella, Ahmed
Boitell, Pedro Luis
Borrego, Orlando
Bosch, Juan
Bretón, Manuel
Brezhnev, Leonid
Bujarin, Nicolai
Bunker, Tamara

Burlanski, Feder
Bustos, Ciro

C
Campanería, Virgilio
Campos, Armando
Candía, Ovando
Carmita
Carretero, Juan
Castro, Fidel
Castro, Manolo
Castro, Raúl
Cienfuegos, Camilo
Chapa, Daniel (alias Coello)
Chaumón, Faure
Chávez, Hugo
Claure, Hilario
Codovilla, Victorio
Coello, Daniel (alias Tuma)
Condori, Casildo (alias Víctor)
Copello Castillo, Lorenzo
Correa, Rafael
Cristo Cuba, Sarabria
Cristo, Jesús
Cubelas, Rolando

D
Debray, Regis
De la Guardia, Antonio
De la Pedraja, Octavio, (alias Moro, Morogoro, El Médico, Tavito)
De la Serna, Celia
Díaz Hascom, Rafael
Díaz Lanz, Pedro Luis
Domínguez Flores, Antonio (alias León)

E
Echeverría, José Antonio

Espín, Vilma
Estela

F
Felipe, León
Fernández, Eufemio
Fernández Caral, Oscar
Fernández Corzo, Rogelio (alias Francisco)
Fernando Montesdeoca, Alberto (alias Pachungo)
Ferrer, Carlos
Ferreira, Chinchina
Fleites, Armando
Franqui, Carlos
Freud, Segismundo
Fricke, Edmond
Fuentes, Norberto

G
Gadea, Hilda
Gómez, Oliveiro
Gorbachov, Mijail
Graham, Alvin
Granado, Alberto
Guerra, Ernesto
Gutierrez, Mario (alias Julio)
Gutierrez Menoyo, Eloy
Guevara, Aliusha
Guevara, Camilo
Guevara, Celia
Guevara, Ernesto
Guevara, Hilda
Guevara Lynch, Ernesto
Guevara, Moisés
Guevara, Juan Martín
Guevara, Roberto
Guzmán, Arturo

H
Hapta, James
Hart, Armando
Hernández Osorio, Miguel (alias Manuel)
Hoare, Mike

I
Illía, Arturo

J
Jiménez Bazán, Orlando (alias Camba)

K
Kabila, Laurent Desiré
Kamenev, Lev
Kasavubu, Joseph
Kennedy, John F.
Kosigyn, Alexei
Kruschev, Nikita
Kuanda, Kenneth

L
Lai, Chou-en
Lendán, Bárbaro
López, Antonio (alias Ñico)
Lumumba, Patrice

M
Mbili
Machín, Gustavo (alias Alejandro)
March, Aleida
Martínez Heredia, Fernando
Martínez, Isaac
Martínez, Jorge Luis
Martínez Tamayo, José María (alias Papi)
Massengo, Idelphose
Masseti, Jorge

Matos, Húber
Mitchel, Leroy
Mena, Adolfo (Che)
Méndez Korne, Julio L. (alias Ñato)
Mesa Lago, Carmelo
Mikoyan, Anastas
Milliard, Roland
Miller, Adrianne
Minná, Giani
Miró Cardona, José
Mobutu, Joseph
Monje, Mario
Morgan, Alexander (alias William)
Montero, Renán (alias Iván)
Mora Morales, Menelao
Mora Valverde, Manuel
Morales, Evo
Mundani, Joseph

N
Nasser, Abdel Gamal
Nkrumah, Kwame
Núñez Tardío, Antonio (alias Pan Divino)

O
Ochoa, Arnaldo
O'Donnell, Pacho
Olmedo, Ricardo
Ortega, Luis

P
País, Agustín
País, Frank
Pantoja, Olo (alias Antonio)
Paz Estensoro, Víctor
Pazos, Felipe
Peredo, Coco

Peredo, Into
Pérez, Faustino
Perón, Juan Domingo
Pesce, Hugo
Petterson, Gerardo
Piñeiro, Manuel (alias Barbarroja)

Q
Quiroga, Horacio
Quispaya Choque, Raúl

R
Ramírez, Porfirio Remberto
Ramos Latour, René (alias Daniel)
Ray, Manuel
Reyes, Eliecer (alias Rolando)
Reyes Rodríguez, Eliseo
Reinaga, Aniceto
Rivera, Héctor
Rocabadas, Vicente
Rodríguez, Félix
Rodríguez, Fructuoso
Rojas, Honorato
Roth, Amber

S
Saldaña, Rodolfo
Salvador, David
Sánchez Díaz, Antonio (alias Pinares)
Santamaría Cuadrado, Haydee
Selich, Andrés
Shelton, Roberto (alias Papi)
Sorí Marín, Humberto
Stalin, Joseph
Suárez Gayol, Jesús (alias El Rubio)

T
Tamayo, Leonardo (alias Ricardo)
Tapia Ruano, Alberto
Terán, Mario
Thompson, Wendell
Touré, Sekou
Trostky, Leon
Tse-Tung, Mao

U
Urrutia, Manuel
Urrutia, Miriam

V
Valdés, Ramiro
Valle Galindo, Fernando
Vazques Viaña, Ricardo (alias Loro)
Villaseca, Arturo
Villegas, Harry (alias Pombo)
Villoldo, Gustavo

W
Walsh, Sinesio

Z
Zenteno, Joaquín

ABOUT THE AUTHOR

Alberto Müller, writer, journalist and author of the book *Why Fidel abandoned Che* and other works, has no qualms about admitting that he sleeps little, drinks to compromise and considers himself a liberal Christian, in the best sense of the word. That is why, after so much traveling through life, he prefers transformations in peace and understanding dialogues, rather than violent confrontations.

He was born in Cuba and confesses that he would like to die on his island.

He speaks openly and honestly about his favorite people: he is passionate about the pure love of Mother Teresa of Calcutta for the helpless; the social genius of Charles Chaplin; the picaresque appeal of Marilyn Monroe; the human ethics of Vaclal Havel; the music of John Lennon; and the theology of poverty of Pope Francis.

He states, with much gratitude, that his master in the art of investigative journalism is the Spaniard journalist Javier Cercas.

The imprint of 15 years of political imprisonment, of having suffered a mock execution and torture on his body - such as

having been forced into a ditch of excrement and beaten —
as well as dreaming of a world of freedom and social justice,
have left this tireless writer with a tenderly watchful gaze.

Among his published books are *Monólogo con Yolanda* (a
novel that falls within the category of magical realism), *Retos
del periodismo* (an essay dedicated to his students of the
subject Laws and Ethics of Journalism at the Koubek Center
of the University of Miami), *Todos heridos por el Norte y por el
Sur* (stories of social structure), *USA: Tierra condenada* (*USA:
Damned Land*) and *Tierra Metalizada* (*Metallized Land*) (two
intimate poetry collections), *El proyecto Varela* (*The Varela
Project*) and *Cuba entre dos extremos* (*Cuba between two
extremes*) (essays on the progress of his Cuban island), make
up a work of impact and show the pressing narrative of the
author.

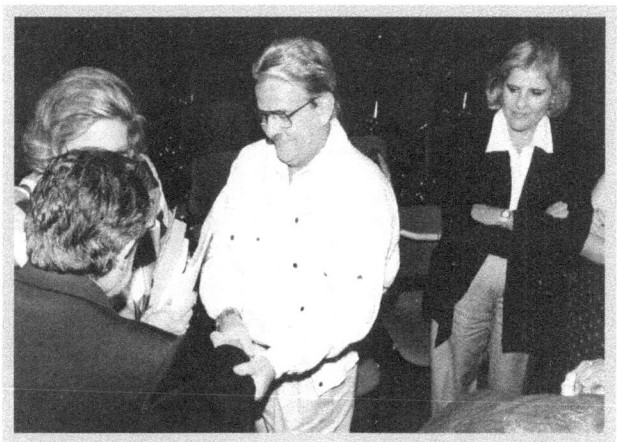

Alberto Müller greeting and chatting with Octavio Paz, winner of the 1990 Nobel Prize in Literature, the only Mexican to win the Nobel Prize in Literature. Behind him is his wife Tensy Müller.

Alberto Müller interviewing Germán Escarrá, a very known politician from Venezuela.

Albeto Müller talking to his good friend and
Cuban writer Guillermo Cabrera Infante.

Alberto Müller interviewing his friend Edén Pastora
of Nicaragua's Comandante O.

Alberto Müller interviewing Pompeyo Márquez,
President of the Communist Party of Venezuela.

Alberto Müller interviewing Miguel Enrique Otero
Silva, Director of the Caracas, Venezuelan
newspaper *El Nacional*.

www.ingramcontent.com/pod-product-compliance
Lightning Source LLC
Chambersburg PA
CBHW051615120626
46551CB00014B/1805